WOK
COOKBOOK

WOK COOKBOOK
Yan-kit So

PIATKUS

To my Mother and to Lady Brunner

Author's acknowledgements

I am indebted to Professor Joseph Needham for
pointing me in the right direction in my research into
the history of the wok, a subject which has been little
explored. Thanks are also due to Mrs Man-tong Yip for
sending me research material from Hong Hong. I also
wish to thank Chef Woo Kwun of Fung Shing
Restaurant in Soho for inspiring several recipes, notably
Stir-fried Whole Scallops, Phoenix Rolls and Smoked
Halibut. Last but not least, I would like to thank my
editor, Gill Cormode, whose sustaining interest not
only in tasting my food but also in trying out some of
the recipes herself made the writing and cooking of
them that much more fun.

© 1985 Yan-kit So

First published in 1985 by
Judy Piatkus (Publishers) Limited, London

Reprinted in 1985
Second Reprint in 1987

British Library Cataloguing in Publication Data
So, Yan-kit
   Wok cookbook.
   1. Wok cookery
   I. Title
   641.5'8   TX840.W65

   ISBN 0–86188–492–2 hardback
        0–86188–322–5 paperback

Design by Paul Saunders
Drawings by Soun Vannithone

Typeset by Phoenix Photosetting, Chatham
Printed and bound by Mackays of Chatham Ltd

CONTENTS

Introduction   6

The Wok   7

Soups   16

Steaming   23

Stir-frying   32

Sautéing   58

Deep-frying   75

Braising   85

References   93

Index   94

Introduction

Of all the many different kinds of Chinese dishes, if not all the foods in the world, I confess that my favourites are those stir-fried in the wok. Such dishes are light, juicy, healthy and, above all, so fragrant that I can never tire of them. It is not surprising, therefore, that in my pursuit of the Chinese culinary art as a cook, teacher, demonstrator and writer, I aspire to make stir-frying my forté, like so many great Chinese chefs. The chopping and cutting up of ingredients is, admittedly, time-consuming and patience-trying, but I accept it as a worthwhile necessity. When it comes to marinating, an essential part of Chinese cooking, I enjoy the mixing of flavours, seemingly at random but really aimed at achieving either a well-balanced result or an emphasis on a particular flavour.

You may well ask why in this book the measurements for the seasonings are so exact, down to the last ¼ if not ⅛ of a teaspoon! Do the Chinese really cook this way? The answer is no. Like all good cooks, they instinctively sprinkle in a pinch of salt, a dash of soy, a bit of sugar and a splash of wine. And yet, if you actually watch them do so, you will note that the 'pinch' and the 'bit' always measure more or less the same. For those new to Chinese cookery who are not familiar with the simple art of mixing those flavours, so essential to the success of Chinese cookery, I have painstakingly worked out the balanced amount for them. But by all means free yourself from my guide-lines and start having fun mixing your own concoctions of flavours. Only by doing so will you become your own expert Chinese cook!

What captures my cookery imagination about stir-frying is the very opera-tion itself. Exhilarating, verging on a sense of theatre, I love also the near explosive sound of the sizzling of the garlic and spring onion and the splash-ing of the wine. When I wield the wok scoop and turn and toss the morsels around in the wok, I feel as if I were a conjuror magically, in the twinkling of an eye, changing the raw pieces into a succulent and fragrant dish.

For me, there is nothing more therapeutic than stirring away in the wok to get rid of any pent-up emotion or tension I may feel, nor is there anything more gratifying than to have a wokful of goodies shared and enjoyed by my family and friends.

Yan-kit So
September 1984, London

THE WOK

The Chinese Wok

The last two decades saw such an increased interest all over the world in Chinese cookery that in the late 1970s 'wok' became an English loanword in the *Collins English Dictionary*. Wok is the Cantonese pronunciation while *Guo* is the *pinyin* Chinese. But in China today, as in the rest of the world, this thin-walled, hemispherical pan, made more often than not of carbon iron than of cast iron, is known as the wok.

The wok's virtues cannot be extolled in sufficient superlatives. It is the most economical and versatile cooking utensil in the world, and its efficacy is difficult to exaggerate. Its wall, as thin as a metal sheet, makes for the quickest transmission of heat resulting in the best economy in fuel consumption and the shortest duration of cooking time. In this one utensil the whole spectrum of Chinese cookery techniques – stir-frying, sautéing, deep-frying, boiling, steaming and even braising to name but the major ones – can be executed. When called upon to perform beyond its Chinese duties, like tossing spaghetti with carbonara sauce or frying Chicken Kiev, it does equally well. So well established is its universal usage in the 1980s that it is not a question of listing which country under the umbrella of the United Nations uses the wok, but rather one of asking which country does not. So popular has it become, especially among the young and health conscious, that department stores vie with each other at Christmas time to sell the largest number of gift wok sets, complete with dome-like covers, rings, scoops and sometimes even brushes and chopsticks.

Archaeological evidence shows that the wok traces its origin to before the Christian era. But it is not easy to chronicle its evolution from its most ancient to its present form. This, no doubt, is partly due to the fact that iron rusts away, and many an ancient wok did not survive. Also, because it was a utilitarian vessel rather than a precious object, it was used much less by the nobility as a burial artefact. The story that has emerged, gleaned from archaeological finds, is fascinating but still leaves intriguing questions unanswered.

The Iron Age began in Greece in about 1200 BC, but it did not begin in China until 500–600 BC, although some authorities would say it started earlier. What is remarkable is that almost as soon as iron was known to the Chinese they discovered the technology of melting and casting it so that by the 4th century BC China was already producing cast iron. Agricultural tools were made and, during the Han dynasty (206 BC to AD 220), cast iron pots, the ancestors of the wok, came into existence. It is worth mentioning that cast iron was not produced in Europe until the late 14th century, and then only in small quantities. Large-scale production did not follow until very early in the 18th century, and the first things made from cast iron were probably cooking vessels.

From the limited number of excavated specimens which have been written about in Chinese archaeological journals, two types of cast iron cooking pot with distinguishing features have been isolated. These are the *fu* (cauldron or pot) and the *guo* (pan or wok). The majority, the *fu*, are about 20 cm high with a round or flat bottom, a curving globular body narrowing upward toward the neck and lip. They may or may not have two looped handles, one on each side of the pot just above the belly.[1] That these iron pots

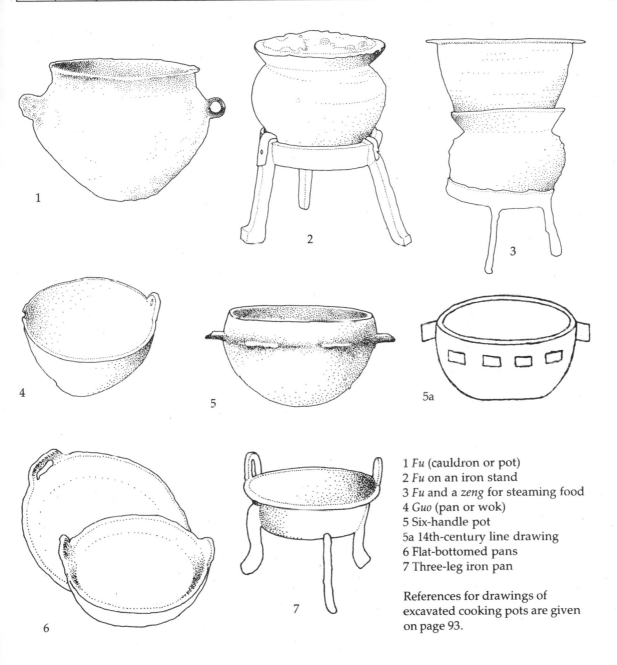

1 *Fu* (cauldron or pot)
2 *Fu* on an iron stand
3 *Fu* and a *zeng* for steaming food
4 *Guo* (pan or wok)
5 Six-handle pot
5a 14th-century line drawing
6 Flat-bottomed pans
7 Three-leg iron pan

References for drawings of excavated cooking pots are given on page 93.

were used for cooking there is little doubt. Some excavated from a Later Han tomb (AD 25–220) still show burn marks and have soot on the outside; at least one was found sitting on a three-leg iron stand,[2] and another holding a clay pot or *zeng* on top for steaming food[3] (see also page 24). It is difficult to ascertain how widely used they were, especially among the common people. The most basic cooking utensil at that time was made of earthenware, for both the rich and the poor, while bronze ware was also in use.

The other type of pot, the *guo*, has a round bottom and is hemispherical in shape with an open and wide rim and two handles. One *guo*, even though it is very small, measuring 8.5 cm in depth and 14 cm across the rim, and with one loop handle missing, looks remarkably like the present-day wok, although it is too deep in proportion to its width across the rim.[4] What is very interesting, though, is that another *guo*, much larger and thicker, was in fact used to smelt bronze for coining money.

During the next six centuries after the Han dynasty there does not seem to be any excavated specimen to chart the development of the cast iron cooking pot.

The next group of specimens, excavated near Peking and in North-east China, notably from historical sites rather than from tombs, date from the 10th to the 14th centuries. The majority are known as six-handle pots, so called because of the six flat, rectangular handles attached at regular intervals around the exterior wall of the pot. Circular and with a round bottom, the pot is deep but is even wider across the rim, which sometimes rolls slightly outward. The largest one, found in North-east China, is 32.3 cm high, 51.5 cm across the rim and 67 cm across the widest

part of the body just where the handles are.[5] These pots were used by rural communities for cooking noodles and pasta food. In the famous 14th-century book, *Work on Agriculture* (Nong Shu), there is a line drawing of the six-handle pot,[5a] which, except for its flat bottom, looks very similar to the excavated specimen.

A parallel development to the six-handle pot is manifest in the double-handle pan, a pair of which were excavated in 1969 near Peking in the same site as the six-handle pot. Both flat-bottomed with soot and burn marks still apparent on the exterior, the pans measure 5.8 cm and 6.6 cm in height against a rim diameter of 39.5 cm and 31 cm respectively. Notably, the iron pans have two handles on opposite sides of the rim, not unlike the present-day wok handles.[6]

Another type of iron pan of the same period is the three-leg pan, shallow, flat-bottomed, having two handles on opposite sides and three legs attached to the base.[7] Obviously, the function of the legs was to allow fuel to be burned underneath the pan.

Both the double-handle and the three-leg pans were probably used for sautéing and for frying cakes, as both their flat bottoms and shallow bodies are conducive to such cookery techniques.

When did the transformation to the present-day wok take place? This question is easier to ask than to answer. One literary reference, reinforced by a charming and convincing illustration of the actual casting of woks on moulds, sheds much light on the subject. In *The Exploitation of the Works of Nature* (Tian Gong Kai Wu) published in 1637, there is a description and a drawing of the manufacturing of cast iron woks *en masse*, not only in China but also in neighbouring

Korea. The size varied, the largest reputedly having a capacity to cook 2 piculs (or more than 250 pounds) of rice, enough to feed 1,000 monks! The measurements of the two standard-sized woks are given as follows: the larger had a rim diameter of about 28 inches (71 cm) and the smaller 14 inches (35 cm), both about ⅓ inch (5 mm) thick. Our modern woks, in comparison, are thinner and lighter. What is so remarkable is that the smaller 14-inch (35-cm) wok is precisely what I use every day and have always recommended as the ideal size for home cooking.

The Wok Set

The multi-purpose lightweight wok, nowadays made of carbon iron, has a round bottom and either two metal or wooden handles or one long wooden handle. It fits over a brazier or a brick stove with fire holes, as found in many homes in China.

To adapt the wok to the standard Western kitchen, it is advisable to acquire a wok set, complete with a lid or cover, a ring or stand and a scoop.

The lid, usually made of aluminium with a wooden knob on top, is sometimes shaped like a round dome and sometimes a plateau dome. The latter, more spacious inside, is preferable, for it covers snugly a whole duck or chicken or a whole fish.

The stand, also metal, often has round holes around it, giving air to the gas flame. For deep-frying, steaming, braising and making soups, when there is a large amount of boiling liquid or hot oil in the wok, it is essential that it sits securely on the stand. But for stir-frying and even sautéing, when the wok can be steadied by one mittened hand, the cooking is done more effectively without the stand.

The scoop, sometimes iron and sometimes stainless steel, looks like a shovel – indeed, such is the Chinese name for it – and it has a long handle with a wooden end for easy holding. Even though it is adequate to use a metal spatula or slice, the wok scoop is constructed at such an angle as to facilitate the turning and tossing motion around the curved sides of the wok.

Personally, I have always preferred round-bottomed woks with two metal or wooden handles, and I have always used gas in my kitchen. Woks come in different sizes, but the 14-inch (35-cm) size is what I use and would recommend for home cooking, for it is both wide enough and deep enough in which to perform all the wok cookery techniques.

An iron wok with sloping sides and a small flat bottom (about 4 inches, 10 cm across) is available for people who cook with electricity. Needless to say, the flat-bottomed wok makes better contact with an electric coil than its round-bottomed counterpart. There are also electric woks which have their own element and a sensitive control knob, and I am told that they also produce a satisfactory result. However, you should stay away from woks made of any metal other than iron, such as aluminium, copper or stainless steel, because they are either too heavy or don't transmit heat as effectively.

Preparing and Caring for the Wok

A new wok has a protective film of grease over it which must be removed before use. To do so, fill the wok with water, add some detergent and boil the water for about half an hour then throw it out. Next scrub the wok hard with an abrasive to rid it of the grease. Now rinse it and dry it over a low heat for about 5 minutes. When it is cool enough to handle, wipe both sides thoroughly with vegetable oil, using either a cloth or kitchen paper. The wok is now ready for cooking.

To clean the wok after each use, wash it with water, using a *mild* detergent if necessary, and a cloth or a soft brush. Do not scrub hard, otherwise you will scratch the surface. Dry thoroughly either over a low heat or with a cloth or kitchen paper and wipe all over again with a small amount of oil. The wok, being iron, rusts easily. The only remedy is to scrub off the rust and wipe over with oil. After a wok has been in constant use for a few months, it becomes well-seasoned, with a dark patina on the surface, and it rusts less easily as long as you keep it dry.

Special Ingredients

Bamboo shoots
Young shoots from the bamboo are cultivated in China for the table. Fresh bamboo shoots are unfortunately seldom if ever available in the West, so that we have no option but to use the canned product. The shoots give a contrast of texture to other ingredients.

Chinese egg noodles
Sold in two forms, fresh or dried, Chinese egg noodles are made of wheat flour, egg and water. Compared with Western noodles, they are more elastic in texture. If they are not available, use noodles from other countries as a substitute.

Cloud ears
Edible tree fungi cultivated in large quantities in Western China. Sold dried, they are black in colour and brittle to the touch. When reconstituted (see page 14), they are used as an absorber of tastes and they lend a slimy yet crunchy texture to other ingredients.

Dried Chinese black mushrooms
Black in appearance, these are specially cultivated tree fungi used as an accompanying ingredient and sometimes as a main ingredient. They lend taste to other ingredients and absorb other tastes, which in turn makes them even more succulent. The Japanese cultivate and supply them to Chinese and Western markets and so they are also well known by the Japanese name *shitake*. They have to be reconstituted before use (see page 14).

Dried shrimps
Orangey pink in colour, their saltiness mitigated by a savoury sweet overtone, and vary-

ing in sizes, they are used as a seasoning for vegetables and soups and in stuffings.

Fermented black beans
These are whole soy beans fermented and preserved in salt and ginger; the dried ones are better than those canned in brine. When combined with garlic and cooked in oil, they become the famous black bean sauce used for a whole range of Chinese dishes.

Five-spice powder
A finely ground golden brown powder made up of five or six spices including star anise, cinnamon, fennel, cloves and Sichuan peppercorns. Used in marinades, it must be used sparingly otherwise it will impart an unpleasant taste to the main ingredient. It is sold in small packets.

Fresh bean curd
Ivory white curd made from ground soy beans and sold in cakes varying in size but commonly 1 inch (2.5 cm) thick and 2½ inches (6.5 cm) square. Very healthy and nutritious, it is one of the most versatile ingredients in Chinese cooking. It is also known by its Japanese name, *tofu*.

Golden needles
This euphemistic name is in reality the term for dried unopened tiger-lily flowers measuring about 3 inches (7.5 cm) in length and looking golden brown in colour. When reconstituted (see page 14), they are used to provide a subtle lightness of texture while they themselves absorb tastes from other ingredients.

Hoisin sauce
Lusciously dark brown, made from soy beans, salt, wheat flour, sugar, vinegar, garlic, chilli and sesame oil resulting in a savoury sweet but tangy taste, it is used both as a seasoning or as a dipping sauce for meats such as roast pork and roast duck. It comes in either bottles or cans.

Oil
The Chinese normally use groundnut oil, but they also use corn oil and vegetable oil.

Oyster sauce
A special Southern Chinese sauce made from extracts of oysters, it is nut brown, usually bottled but sometimes also canned. Less strong than soy sauce but three if not four times more expensive, its special value lies in the sweet and 'meaty' taste it lends to other ingredients whether meat, vegetables, rice or noodles. It is used as a dipping sauce or as a finishing touch to a sauce mixture.

Pickled salty and sour plums
These come in a jar and can be bought at your nearest Chinese store.

Raw frozen prawns
Prawn dishes are an important feature in the Chinese cuisine, and they are always prepared from their raw state, just as meat and fish dishes are. In the West, more often than not, the prawns sold at the fishmonger's are already boiled and are thus not suitable for Chinese cooking. Fortunately, frozen raw prawns are available in Chinese and Oriental stores as well as at some fishmongers, and I would strongly advise trying to get them.

Rice vinegar
Clear and mild vinegar made from rice. White wine vinegar can act as a substitute.

Shaoxing wine
Amber coloured Chinese wine made from glutinous rice, used both for drinking and for cooking. For drinking, it tastes much better

slightly warmed; for cooking, a medium dry sherry can be used as a good substitute.

Sichuan peppercorns

Otherwise known as *fagara*, these small, reddish brown peppercorns are a special product of Sichuan province in Western China. Not as burning hot as black peppercorns, they produce a slight numbing effect made more enticing by their aroma. They are used in stews and braised dishes.

Soy sauce

Made from fermented, protein-rich soy beans, this is an indispensable seasoning to Chinese cooking. There are two main kinds, the thick and the thin, or the dark and the light, both of which are used in Chinese homes and restaurants. Thick soy sauce is darker in colour, thicker in consistency and less salty in taste, while thin soy sauce is lighter, thinner and more salty. Often they are used together in conjunction with salt, but since thick soy sauce gives a reddish brown hue to food, do not use it in marinating or seasoning ingredients when a light appearance is called for. Soy sauce is usually packaged in bottles but also comes in cans.

Star anise

The French use anise seeds in their cooking but the Chinese use the whole, eight-segmented, hard spice with its liquorice taste to flavour their stews and braised dishes. Reddish brown in colour, it does resemble a star, hence its name.

Thickening

In Chinese cooking a range of thickening agents are used: arrowroot, tapioca flour, water chestnut flour, potato flour and cornflour, but the last two are more common and easily available. Compared to cornflour, potato flour is more gelatinous and gives a more subtle and glossy finish to a sauce, but because it is more gelatinous, the quantity used must be less than for cornflour.

Wonton skins

Thin as skin and usually about 3 inches (7.5 cm) square, these wonton wrappers are made of wheat, egg and water. Sold fresh in plastic bags in Chinese stores, they can be frozen.

Special Techniques

To reconstitute a dried ingredient

Dried products, such as Chinese black mushrooms, cloud ears and golden needles, have to be reconstituted in order to return them to their former pliable state. To do this, soak them for 20 minutes or longer in enough hot water for them to expand fully. Then remove them from the soaking liquid, squeeze out excess water but leave them damp. The soaking liquid for the black mushrooms can be reserved for the stockpot or for sauce, but the liquid for cloud ears and golden needles should be dispensed with.

There is often fine sand or other impurities attached to cloud ears and it is therefore advisable to rub them gently once they have expanded in the soaking liquid, plucking off at the same time the hard knobs found on them. As for golden needles, simply chop off the small hard ends after removing them from the liquid.

To make spiced salt

Many Chinese dishes, such as Lemon Chicken (page 68) and Crispy Skin Bean Curd (page 84) benefit from being dipped in a little spiced salt. It enhances the flavour of the food.

To prepare the spiced salt, heat the wok over a medium heat until hot but not smoking. Add 2 tablespoons salt and stir continuously for about 4–5 minutes or until very hot and slightly greyish in colour. Remove to a small bowl, add 1 teaspoon five-spice powder and ½ teaspoon ground white or black pepper. Mix well and serve in small saucers at the table.

To make ginger juice
While the Chinese adore fish, they abhor the fishy odour and believe that ginger counters this odour most effectively.

To prepare ginger juice, peel a large chunk of fresh ginger root, mince it finely or grate it, and then squeeze out the juice with your hand into a container. Discard the pulp. The juice keeps for a long time if refrigerated.

To make a small amount, see Chinese Broccoli with Ginger Juice, page 53, step 3.

How Much to Serve

Unless otherwise stated, every dish in this book yields about six helpings. The Chinese always share the dishes, which are put on the table together. Even a piece of fish, such as a fish steak, would be broken up with chopsticks and everyone would help themselves. For an everyday meal I would suggest making two, and at the most three, dishes to serve four people.

Rice
Rice is the staple food for the Chinese on a national basis, although noodles and steamed breads and buns are just as important a staple food for people in Northern China. All Chinese dishes are eaten with rice, plain boiled as a rule. But by all means serve some of the dishes in this book with noodles, spaghetti, potatoes or whatever staple food takes your fancy.

SOUPS

It may sound ridiculous to make soups in the wok, but the Chinese actually do, and with remarkable success. To be sure, they also use ordinary deep saucepans to make soups and sometimes they combine the use of both. For example, the stock may be made in a saucepan and then the soup made with some of the stock in a wok.

It may be as well to clarify what a Chinese soup is. Unlike a Western soup, which is often quite thick and cream-based, a Chinese soup is basically a thin clear broth with or without some ingredients swimming in it. The most used ingredients are vegetables, either chopped up or sliced, sometimes seasoned with small pieces of meat or fish. For instance, a Chinese cook may use meaty spare ribs as a base and add a few Chinese mushrooms and, in the old days, would have added a little bit 'from the sea', such as the dried *abalone* which is now so expensive that it is out of the reach of most people's pockets. Water would be added and the soup simmered for a couple of hours. If a soup is not tasty enough it is sprinkled with a little (one or two teaspoons) of the magical soy sauce.

The Chinese love to have a bowl of soup with every meal. In the Western sequence of serving a meal, the soup always precedes the main course. In the Chinese sequence, a bowl of clear broth may be put side by side with a bowl of rice for day-to-day family fare. An exotic soup, such as the classic Shark's Fin or Bird's Nest, may come several courses down the line in a banquet. Then again there may be another soup, the clear broth kind, a few dishes after the exotic soup.

In the Chinese home you would never see many of the soups served in Chinese restaurants abroad, such as the immensely popular Wonton Soup. The Chinese would consider wonton (which are rather similar to pork ravioli) as dumplings in a broth, to be eaten for lunch or as a snack!

Mussels in Soup

2½–3 lb (1.2–1.4 kg) mussels
4 tablespoons vegetable oil
2–3 cloves garlic, peeled and roughly
  chopped
1½–2 inches (4–5 cm) fresh ginger
  root, sliced, peeled and well bruised
2 shallots, peeled and roughly chopped
1 large onion, peeled and roughly
  chopped
8 fl oz (225 ml, 1 cup) white wine
  (preferably Sauternes) or cider
¼ teaspoon salt, or to taste
white pepper to taste
small bunch coriander leaves for
  garnish, trimmed

The wok with its wide hemispherical shape is most conducive to cooking mussels, for it allows plenty of room for the mussels to cook and open quickly, and thus stay very juicy. If you like the taste of ginger at all, you will find the accompanying soup, marked by a subtle ginger and wine flavour, agreeable indeed.

1. Scrub and wash the mussels thoroughly, one by one, until they are very clean. Pull off the 'beards' between the shells and knock off the barnacles with the back of a knife. Discard the mussels which are broken or remain open when you tap them. Put in a colander to drain.
2. Heat the wok over a high heat until smoke rises. Add the oil and swirl it around several times. Add the garlic, let sizzle and take on colour, then add the ginger and stir until its aroma is released. Add the shallot and stir for a few more seconds. Lower the heat and add the onion. Stir and cook for about 5 minutes or until the onion is soft. Turn up the heat again, pour in the wine or cider, bring to a fast boil and reduce it by about one-fourth. Season with the salt and pepper.
3. Place the wok on its stand to make it more steady. Pour in the mussels. Sliding the wok scoop or a spatula to the bottom of the wok, give several sweeping turns. Add the wok lid and continue to cook over a moderately high heat for about 4 minutes or until the mussels are wide open, indicating that they are cooked. Discard those which remain closed.
4. Remove the wok from the heat. Scoop the mussels and the accompanying soup into a large soup tureen. Arrange the coriander leaves on top and serve immediately.

Beef Meat Ball Soup

8 oz (225 g) minced beef
2½ pints (1.4 litres, 6¼ cups) lightly-
  seasoned beef or chicken stock
2 tablespoons vegetable oil
6 oz (175 g) fresh mushrooms,
  trimmed and cut into thin slices
2–3 spring onions, green parts only,
  cut into tiny rounds
salt and pepper to taste

FOR THE MARINADE
¼ teaspoon salt
small pinch sugar
1 teaspoon thin soy sauce
2 teaspoons thick soy sauce
8–10 turns black pepper mill
1–1½ teaspoons minced fresh ginger
  root
2 teaspoons Shaoxing wine or medium
  dry sherry
1½ teaspoons potato flour or 2
  teaspoons cornflour
5–6 tablespoons water
1 teaspoon sesame oil
1 tablespoon vegetable oil

A soup sufficiently filling and nourishing to be served as lunch for four people. Although Chinese to the core, it will go very well with French bread. Try it.

1. Marinate the beef. Put the beef in a large mixing bowl. Add the salt, sugar, soy sauces, pepper, ginger, wine or sherry and stir to mix. Sprinkle with the flour, then add the water, 1 tablespoon at a time, and stir vigorously in the same direction until completely absorbed before adding another spoonful. Pick up the whole lump of beef and throw it back into the bowl 50–60 times. This makes the beef light and slippery in texture. Leave in the refrigerator for 30 minutes or longer. Blend in the oils.
2. With your fingers, pick up about 2–3 teaspoons of the meat and roll it into a ball about the size of a ping-pong ball. Repeat with all the beef.
3. Pour the stock into the wok and bring it to the boil. Add the oil. Add the mushrooms and cook over a gentle heat for 4–5 minutes. Add the meat balls. Return the soup to a fast simmer, then continue to cook for about 1½ minutes if you like the beef balls to be pink in the centre, or 2 minutes or longer if you like them to be well done, stirring them around a couple of times. Add the spring onion, give the soup another big stir then remove from the heat.
4. Taste the soup for seasoning. Ladle the meat balls and soup either into a large soup tureen or into individual bowls. Serve hot.

West Lake Beef Soup

6 oz (175 g) beef, rump or fillet, trimmed and cut across the grain into rectangular slices about ½ × 1¼ inches (1 × 3 cm) and ⅕ inch (5 mm) thick
1½ pints (900 ml, 4 cups) unseasoned chicken stock
¼ teaspoon salt, or to taste
2 tablespoons vegetable oil
1 bunch, about 4 oz (100 g), watercress, trimmed, washed and well drained

FOR THE MARINADE
½ teaspoon salt
½ teaspoon sugar
2 teaspoons thin soy sauce
6–8 turns white pepper mill
1½ teaspoons Shaoxing wine or medium dry sherry
1½ teaspoons potato flour or 2 teaspoons cornflour
1 tablespoon water
1 small egg white
1 teaspoon sesame oil
1 tablespoon vegetable oil

This soup purports to celebrate the picturesque and most famous lake in China, the West Lake, not too far away from Shanghai. To be absolutely correct, a small amount of only the leaves of watercress should float on the soup's misty surface, which is caused by the use of egg white. But I have used the stalk of the watercress as well because I don't see any point in wasting such a precious and delicious vegetable. If there is no watercress, just use some individual leaves of coriander, good for decoration and taste. Coriander is a little stronger than broad-leaf parsley or, in Italian, *cilantro*.

1. Marinate the beef. Add the salt, sugar, soy sauce, pepper, wine or sherry and flour to the beef and stir in the same direction to coat. Add the water and stir again until absorbed. Add the egg white, stirring again. Leave to stand in the refrigerator for 15–30 minutes. Blend in the oils.
2. Pour the stock into the wok and bring to a simmer. Add the salt and the oil. Add the beef, stir generously a couple of times with a pair of bamboo chopsticks or a wooden spoon and return to a simmer. Remove at once from the heat. The beef is still slightly underdone in the centre and very tender. Submerge the watercress in the soup. Ladle either into a large soup tureen or individual soup bowls. Serve immediately.

Soup Noodles with Shredded Pork

12 oz (350 g) lean pork, cut into
matchstick-size strips
12 oz (350 g) dried, or 1 lb (450 g)
fresh, Chinese egg noodles
2½ pints (1.4 litres, 6¼ cups) lightly-
seasoned chicken stock
5 tablespoons vegetable oil
3 spring onions, trimmed and cut into
1-inch (2.5-cm) sections, white and
green parts separated
4–6 large leaves Iceberg or Cos lettuce,
torn into pieces
black or white pepper
thin or thick soy sauce

FOR THE MARINADE
½ teaspoon salt
¼ teaspoon sugar
1 tablespoon thin soy sauce
6 turns white pepper mill
1 teaspoon Shaoxing wine or medium
dry sherry
1 teaspoon potato flour or 1⅓
teaspoons cornflour
1 tablespoon water
1 teaspoon sesame oil

Noodles in a clear stock, topped by some meat or sea-food and a few leaf vegetables, are eaten as a light meal from morning to night by many Chinese. It is served as much in noodle eating-houses and street stalls as at home. You can vary the ingredients, using chicken, beef, prawn or crab meat and other vegetables.

1. Marinate the pork. Add the salt, sugar, soy sauce, pepper, wine or sherry, potato flour or cornflour and water to the pork and stir to mix well. Leave to stand for 15–20 minutes, then blend in the oil.
2. Fill the wok with about 4 pints (2.3 litres, 10 cups) of water and bring to the boil. Add the noodles and return to the boil. Using a pair of chopsticks or a fork, separate the noodles and continue to boil until *al dente*. Fresh noodles take about 1½ minutes, dry ones about 3–4 minutes or longer. (Check the packet for instructions.) Pour into a colander to drain. Divide the noodles into 6 portions. Put 1 portion into each of 4 individual bowls, and the remaining 2 portions into a large serving bowl for second helpings.
3. Add the stock to the wok and bring to a gentle boil. Add 3 tablespoons of the oil and the white spring onion. Add the pork, separate with chopsticks or fork and simmer for 45–60 seconds or until opaque. Using a perforated spoon, lift about one-sixth of the pork and white onion each time and place on the noodles in the 4 bowls. Add the remainder to the large bowl.
4. Return the soup to the boil and add the remaining 2 tablespoons oil. Add the lettuce and the green spring onion, return to a gentle boil, then remove the wok from the heat. Divide the lettuce and spring onion as before.
5. Ladle the soup proportionally into the individual bowls and the large bowl and serve immediately. Pepper and soy sauce can be used at the table to individual taste.

Shredded Pork Soup

4 oz (100 g) trimmed lean pork, best
  shoulder or leg, cut into rectangular
  slices about $\frac{1}{2} \times 1\frac{1}{2}$ inches (1 ×
  4 cm) and $\frac{1}{10}$ inch (2 mm) thick
$1\frac{1}{2}$–2 pints (1–1.1 litres, $4\frac{1}{2}$–5 cups)
  unseasoned chicken stock
$1\frac{1}{2}$ tablespoons vegetable oil
$\frac{1}{4}$–$\frac{1}{2}$ teaspoon salt, or to taste
4 oz (100 g) fresh mushrooms,
  trimmed and cut into thin slices
4 stalks coriander leaves (branches of
  leaves only)

FOR THE MARINADE
$\frac{1}{4}$–$\frac{1}{3}$ teaspoon salt
2 teaspoons thin soy sauce
4 turns white pepper mill
1 teaspoon Shaoxing wine or medium
  dry sherry
$\frac{3}{4}$ teaspoon potato flour or 1 teaspoon
  cornflour
$\frac{1}{2}$ tablespoon water
1 teaspoon sesame oil
1 teaspoon vegetable oil

The fresh mushroom adds a sweetness to the chicken-based stock, while the coriander leaves lend an overall fragrance to the soup. Even so, to make the soup truly delicious, the pork slices must be tender and not over-cooked. An even simpler way to make this soup is to use shredded ham. Obviously, with ham there is no need to marinate the meat. If you want to make a more substantial soup, you could add a handful of Chinese noodles or small Italian pasta shapes.

1. Marinate the pork. Add the salt, soy sauce, pepper, wine or sherry and potato flour or cornflour to the pork and stir to coat. Add the water and stir again until well absorbed. Leave to stand for about 15–20 minutes. Blend in the oils.
2. Pour the stock into the wok and bring it to a gentle boil. Add the oil and the salt. Add the mushroom and continue to cook for 4–5 minutes, maintaining a gentle boil.
3. Add the pork, separate the pieces with chopsticks or a fork and return to a gentle boil, continuing to cook for another minute or until the pork is just cooked, having turned opaque. Remove the wok from·the heat. Check the soup for seasoning. Immerse the coriander leaves into the soup before scooping into either a large soup tureen or individual bowls. Serve immediately.

STEAMING

What's so special about Chinese steaming is that all the goodness and taste of the ingredients are retained, whereas one associates Western steaming with tastelessness. The method of steaming is as follows. Place the wok on its stand on top of the burner. Put either a metal trivet or a small bamboo cage upside down in the centre of the wok. Put whatever food is to be steamed on a shallow heatproof dish, so that the juices are retained in the dish when the food is cooked. Put the dish on the metal or bamboo stand. Next, fill the wok with boiling water to about 1 inch (2.5 cm) of the base of the dish in order to prevent the bubbling water from getting into the dish and spoiling the food. Add the wok lid, turn up the heat, maintaining it at the same intensity to ensure that plenty of steam rises from the boiling water and circulates inside the covered wok to cook the food. If the food is to be steamed for a long time, as is the case for a duck, be sure to replenish the water from time to time. A piece of fish, however, cooks through very quickly. Another small but important point to bear in mind is this: refrain from lifting the wok lid unnecessarily, for every time you do so steam escapes and you will need to steam the food for a longer period in order to make sure it is cooked.

Steaming is one of the oldest cookery techniques in China, dating back at least 4,000 years. It was done in a primitive yet, for its time, most sophisticated steamer made of pottery or bronze. The base, called the *li*, was a cooking pot with three breast-shaped hollow legs which sat over a fire and in which water could be boiled or rice cooked. On top of the *li* stood a vessel called a *zeng*, which had a perforated flat bottom, the design of which is hardly changed today, through which steam came up to cook the food inside. This principle of steaming food has always remained the same, while the wok has long since become a substitute for the *li*.

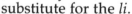

li

zeng and *fu*

Steamed Siu Mai

1 lb (450 g) shelled and deveined small
   raw prawns, pat dried and coarsely
   minced
1¼ teaspoons salt
1 lb (450 g) trimmed lean pork, leg
   joint, fairly finely minced
10 medium-sized dried Chinese
   mushrooms, reconstituted (see page
   14) and fairly finely minced
2 tablespoons thin soy sauce
1¼ teaspoons sugar
10 turns white pepper mill
2 tablespoons vegetable oil
1–2 teaspoons sesame oil
50–60 pieces wonton skin, each about
   3 inches (7.5 cm) square (see page
   14)

One of the most basic Cantonese *dimsum* (hors d'oeuvres) is *siu mai*, open-topped pork dumplings. It is worth your trouble and expense to get the raw prawn rather than use just pork, as so many restaurants seem to do these days.

1. Prepare the stuffing. Put the minced prawn into a large bowl. Add the salt and, using either a pair of chopsticks or a fork, stir vigorously in the same direction for about 2 minutes or until the prawn has become gelatinous. Add the minced pork and Chinese mushroom, then add the soy sauce, sugar and pepper. Stir in the same direction again for another 2–3 minutes until the mixture is gelatinous. Leave to stand for about 15–20 minutes. Stir in the oils.

2. Wrap the *siu mai*. Clip off the four corner triangles of 1 piece of wonton skin, then place it between the fingertips and the palm of one hand. Put about 1 table-spoon of stuffing on the centre of the skin. Close the hand, squeezing the skin gently into an upright pouch, the skin forming natural pleats around the stuffing. Using a small knife, smooth down the stuffing to level with the top of the skin pleats, and squeeze gently to form a neck and ensure the stuffing remains stuck to the skin throughout the steaming. Stand the 'pouches' on a flat surface to give them a flat bottom. Repeat until the stuffing is used up.

3. Steam the *siu mai*. Space them out on either an oiled bamboo steaming cage or a heatproof dish placed on a trivet and steam in the wok, covered, until cooked. In a bamboo cage, the steaming time is 5–6 minutes, while in a dish 7–8. Serve piping hot.

Note: Siu mai can be prepared in advance and also frozen either before or after steaming.

Steamed Fish

1 grey mullet about 2 lb (900 g),
  cleaned (about 1½ lb, 700 g after
  cleaning) but with the head left on;
  or about 1¼ lb (550 g) fish steak,
  halibut, turbot or cod, about
  ¾–1 inch (2–2.5 cm) thick
½ inch (1 cm) fresh ginger, peeled and
  finely shredded
4 large spring onions, trimmed and
  cut into 2-inch (5-cm) sections then
  finely shredded, white and green
  parts separated
3–4 tablespoons vegetable oil
2½ tablespoons thick soy sauce
white pepper to taste

The Chinese hanker after steamed fish much as the Westerners are predisposed to beef steaks. The choicer and fresher the fish, the more likely it will be steamed rather than cooked in any other way. Sea bass is superb for steaming, so are Dover sole and halibut and turbot steaks, but rainbow trout, grey mullet, lemon sole and haddock or even cod steak are subtly delicious. The key is to steam it just to a turn without overcooking it.

To steam a fish 'clear', only ginger and spring onion are used; otherwise, the most usual condiment is the versatile black beans spread on the fish and steamed with it. If a fish or fish steak is too long for the heatproof dish on which it is steamed, halve it and put the pieces side by side. When cooked, add this finishing touch: pour over it a small amount of hot oil and add some soy sauce which, mixed with the natural juices from the fish, will make a flavourful sauce.

1. Rinse the fish and pat dry. Halve crosswise. Put the two pieces side by side on a heatproof dish with raised edges. Spread the ginger on top and put some in the cavity.
2. Place the dish on the trivet in the wok and steam (see page 24), tightly covered, over a high heat for 8–10 minutes or until the fish turns opaque, the flesh barely coming away from the main bone.
3. Remove the lid. If too much liquid formed by the steam is found on the dish around the fish, dab some off with kitchen paper. Spread the green then the white spring onion on the fish. (For those who like their spring onion more cooked, they can replace the lid and steam for 30–60 seconds.)
4. Heat the oil in a small saucepan until smoke rises. Pour it on the spring onion, dribbling it down slowly so that the sizzling oil partially cooks the spring onion.
5. Pour the soy sauce over the fish and season with pepper to taste. Serve immediately.

Steamed Minced Pork

12 oz (350 g) minced pork
4–6 medium dried Chinese
    mushrooms, reconstituted (see page
    14) and minced
2–3 oz (50–75 g) canned bamboo
    shoots or 6–8 canned water
    chestnuts, minced
4 spring onions, cut into small
    rounds, white and green parts
    separated
2 tablespoons vegetable oil
1–2 teaspoons sesame oil

FOR THE MARINADE
½ teaspoon salt
½ teaspoon sugar
2 teaspoons thin soy sauce
8 turns white pepper mill
2 teaspoons Shaoxing wine or medium
    dry sherry
1 teaspoon potato flour or 1⅓
    teaspoons cornflour
4 tablespoons chicken stock

A typical family dish for everyday consumption. The addition of dried Chinese mushroom and bamboo shoots or water chestnut to the pork makes the texture particularly pleasing to the palate. When cooked it looks like a large meat patty. What the Chinese do is use thin chopsticks and lift away one bite-sized chunk at a time. You may prefer to cut it into small pieces with a knife first.

1. Marinate the pork. Add the salt, sugar, soy, pepper and wine or sherry to the pork and mix well. Sprinkle with the potato flour or cornflour, add the stock, 1 tablespoon at a time, stirring in the same direction until completely absorbed before adding another spoonful. This makes the pork fluffy and light. Leave to stand for 15–20 minutes.
2. Add the Chinese mushroom, bamboo shoots or water chestnut and white spring onion to the pork and mix evenly. Stir in the vegetable oil and sesame oil.
3. Spread this mixture on to a round heatproof serving dish, about 8–10 inches (20–25 cm) in diameter with slightly raised edges. Put the dish into the wok and steam (see page 24), covered tightly, over a high heat for 8–10 minutes or until the pork is cooked. There will be some juice on the pork. Lift the wok cover, sprinkle on the green spring onion and put the cover on again and steam for about 5 seconds. Remove the dish and serve immediately.

Steamed Beef with Bamboo Shoots

12 oz (350 g) trimmed rump or skirt
   steak, cut into slices about
   1 × 1½ inches (2.5 × 4 cm) and
   ¼ inch (6 mm) thick
4 oz (100 g) canned bamboo shoots, cut
   into thin slices
3–4 spring onions, cut into 1-inch
   (2.5-cm) sections, white and green
   parts separated
1–2 tablespoons oil

FOR THE MARINADE
1 inch (2.5 cm) fresh ginger root,
   peeled and finely chopped
½ teaspoon salt
¼ teaspoon sugar
1½ tablespoons thick soy sauce
8 turns black pepper mill
2 teaspoons Shaoxing wine or medium
   dry sherry
1½ teaspoons potato flour or 2
   teaspoons cornflour
1 tablespoon water
1½ tablespoons vegetable oil
1 teaspoon sesame oil

This family dish is so succulent that it is also fit for the most special of guests. Just like roast beef or steak, you can have it anything from well done to rare, depending on how you like it.

The bamboo shoots, intent on giving a contrast of texture to the tender beef, can be substituted by a few mushrooms sliced very thinly.

Here I give one way of making ginger juice. The master recipe on page 15 is ideal for large quantities and for those who cook Chinese food all the time.

1. Marinate the beef. In 2–3 batches, put the ginger in a garlic press, add 2–3 drops of water each time and squeeze the resulting juice on to the beef, scraping in the minced ginger on the press as well, discarding the pulp inside. Add the salt, sugar, soy sauce, pepper, wine or sherry and flour and stir until well coated. Add the water and stir again. Leave to stand for about 20–30 minutes. Blend in the oils.
2. Mix the bamboo shoots into the beef.
3. Spread the beef mixture over a heatproof dish with raised edges. Scatter the white spring onion on top. Put the dish into the wok and steam (see page 24), covered, for about 4–5 minutes. The beef should be either just done or slightly underdone, depending on personal taste. Remove the wok cover, mix the beef to ensure the flour is well cooked, then scatter on the green spring onion. Steam, covered, for another 30–45 seconds. Remove the dish. Heat the oil in a small saucepan until smoke rises and pour it on to the beef. Serve preferably from the same dish.

Steamed Chicken Fillet

10–12 oz (275–350 g) chicken breast fillet without skin, cut into pieces about ½ inch (1 cm) wide
4–5 oz (100–150 g) fresh white mushrooms, trimmed and cut into ¼-inch (6-mm) slices
4 thin slices fresh ginger root, peeled
4–6 spring onions, cut into 1-inch (2.5-cm) sections

FOR THE MARINADE
½ teaspoon salt
½ teaspoon sugar
1 tablespoon thin soy sauce
6 turns white pepper mill
2 teaspoons Shaoxing wine or medium dry sherry
2 teaspoons cornflour
1½ tablespoons egg white
2½–3 tablespoons vegetable oil
1 teaspoon sesame oil

Steamed chicken is regular family fare for the Chinese. As often as not, the chicken is cut up into pieces through the skin and bones (see Variation), for the Chinese love to chew around the bones, believing that the meat around them is more succulent and tasty than white meat. Try both the recipe and the variation and judge for yourself. You may like it both ways.

1. Marinate the chicken in a bowl. Add the salt, sugar, soy sauce, pepper, wine or sherry, cornflour and egg white to the chicken and mix to coat evenly. Leave to stand for about 15 minutes. Stir in the oils. Add the mushroom and mix with the chicken.
2. Transfer the mixture on to a heatproof plate with raised sides, spreading out into a single layer if possible. Scatter the ginger and spring onion on top.
3. Steam in the wok (see page 24) for about 8 minutes until the chicken is cooked, having turned white. There will be juice around the chicken from the steaming, which is delicious. Remove from the wok and serve preferably straight from the same plate.

VARIATION: *Steamed Drumsticks and Wings*

3 drumsticks
3 wings

Chop each drumstick through the skin and bone with a cleaver into 3 pieces. Joint the wings and halve each section. Proceed as above and steam the chicken for about 15 minutes until cooked.

Steamed Duck with a Plum Sauce

1 × 4–4½ lb (1.8–2 kg) oven-ready
   duck, oil sacs removed and
   discarded
1 large kettle boiling water
1 teaspoon thick soy sauce
1 tablespoon vegetable oil
vinegar to taste
1½ tablespoons Shaoxing wine or
   medium dry sherry
several teaspoons potato flour or
   cornflour

FOR THE PLUM SAUCE DRESSING
6 oz (175 g) pickled salty and sour
   plums
1–2 tablespoons own liquid from the
   jar
3–4 tablespoons sugar
1 teaspoon salt

This dish finds special favour with the Cantonese during the summer months when it is very humid and hot in sub-tropical South China. The sweet and sour plum sauce reduces the grease of the duck and rouses people's appetite to eat even in the heat.

1. Prepare the plum sauce dressing. Pit the plums (reserving the stones) and mash with the liquid. Add the sugar and salt.
2. Scald the duck with boiling water. As the water is poured over the skin, it shrinks and becomes shiny. Wipe off excess water. While the skin is still warm, brush all over with the soy sauce to add colour.
3. Heat the wok over a high heat until smoke rises. Add the oil and swirl it around. Add the duck breast side down and brown for 45–60 seconds. Turn over to brown the back and then the two sides in the same way. Remove and discard the oil. Wash the wok and set it up for steaming (see page 24).
4. Place the duck in a heatproof dish with raised sides. Spread the plum dressing and half of the pits over the skin; put the remaining pits inside the cavity. Steam for about 1½ hours until the duck is tender, replenishing the water in the wok 2–3 times.
5. Remove the duck to another dish and scrape the plum dressing into a saucepan. Discard the pits. Spoon off most of the fat on the liquid in the heatproof dish, then pour the liquid into the saucepan. Test for taste and add a little vinegar, and more salt and sugar if necessary. Add the wine or sherry. Slowly bring to a simmer and thicken with either potato flour or cornflour, allowing 1 teaspoon potato flour or 1⅓ teaspoons cornflour dissolved in 1 tablespoon water for every 3 fl oz (85 ml) sauce. Keep the sauce hot.
6. Either chop the duck through the bones into 1-inch (2.5-cm) pieces the Chinese way or carve it. Pour over the plum sauce and serve immediately.

Steamed Rice

2 cups or about 13 oz (375 g)
   long-grain white rice
2 cups or 16 fl oz (450 ml) water
1 tablespoon vegetable oil

Rice is the staple food for the Chinese and can be eaten with every dish in the book. Long-grain white rice – husked and polished – is what the Chinese like to eat every single day. It is as traditional to boil rice as it is to steam it but, whereas boiled rice has a tendency to stick together, steamed rice is firmer in texture and the grains are more separate. To steam rice, use the same volume of water as rice, for example 1 cup of rice and 1 cup of water. One cup of uncooked rice yields about 3 loose cups of cooked rice.

This recipe is the basis for more fancy rice dishes, such as Shrimp Stir-fried Rice and Mixed Fried Rice (see pages 49 and 50).

1. Wash the rice in several changes of water, rubbing with the fingers, until the water is no longer milky. Drain off excess water. (This can also be done in a wire sieve under running water.)
2. Put the rice in either a cake tin or a Pyrex pie dish. Add the water and oil. Put the tin or dish on the steaming stand in the wok.
3. Steam, covered, over a high heat for about 25 minutes in a cake tin or 35 minutes in a Pyrex dish, at the end of which time the rice should be firm but cooked through. Fluff up the rice and serve. It yields about 6 loose cups of rice.

STIR-FRYING

Preparing raw ingredients for stir-frying.

Beef with Mange-tout (Stir-frying: page 39).

Prawns in Black Bean Sauce
(Stir-frying: page 38).

Shredded Pork with Cucumber and Stir-fried Mixed Vegetables (Stir-frying: pages 43 and 57).

As a technique in Chinese cookery, stir-frying came later than boiling, steaming, stewing and roasting on a spit. Yet it is the most ingenious technique which has captured the imagination of the whole world, so much so that many people regard it as synonymous with Chinese cuisine.

The technique consists of adding cut up ingredients to an intensely heated wok containing a small amount of oil, then turning and tossing them around the curved sides until they are cooked just to a turn, with most of the vitamins still intact. This method can be used for cooking any foodstuff, be it vegetable, meat, seafood or rice and noodles. Vegetables stir-fried are crisp and crunchy, meat and seafood are tender and juicy, but above all, they are impregnated down to the last morsel with a special fragrance the Chinese unashamedly term 'wok fragrance'.

How to achieve the best stir-fried results? A closer look at the process reveals the clues. The ingredients are always cut up into more or less uniform sizes so that they are cooked at the same time. Pieces of meat more often than not are marinated so that the mixed flavours, interacting with the oil and the condiments, permeate each morsel. The wok itself is always heated until it is red-hot before oil is poured in and swirled around. The oil is then seasoned by one or two if not all three of the basic condiments – ginger, garlic and spring onion, sometimes known as the Chinese trinity in the kitchen. Speed, instant control of heat and dexterous turning and tossing of the ingredients in the wok, if not actually tossing them in mid-air as so dramatically performed by professional male Chinese chefs, are the next essential steps so that the ingredients can be cooked quickly without becoming tough or soggy. Although not absolutely necessary, the splashing in of a small amount of alcohol enhances the fragrance as the food sizzles in the wok. The addition of a simple sauce, usually soy sauce based with a tiny amount of dissolved thickening, completes the operation. And we have a healthy, delicious and fragrant dish to eat!

Stir-fried Vegetables

Needless to say, the wok is the best utensil in which to stir-fry vegetables, especially leaf vegetables, resulting in crunchy texture, full retention of vitamins and nutrition, flavourful tastes and mouth-watering fragrance. Heat the wok over a high heat, add the oil then the ginger and white spring onion and stir several times to release their aroma. Add the vegetable and toss and turn until cooked, seasoning with salt and soy sauce (or oyster sauce) if used and adjusting the heat if necessary. Add the green spring onion towards the end of cooking. Below is a chart to give further guidelines.

Vegetable	Vegetable oil	Condiments	Seasoning	Stir-frying time
1 lb (450 g) bean sprouts	3–4 tablespoons	3 slices peeled fresh ginger root; 2–3 spring onions, cut into 1-inch (2.5-cm) sections, white and green parts separated	½ teaspoon salt, 2 teaspoons thin soy sauce	3 minutes over high heat throughout
1½ lb (700 g) Chinese leaf shredded crosswise at ½-inch (1-cm) intervals, the stalk cooked first for 2 minutes	4 tablespoons	3 slices peeled fresh ginger root; 2–3 spring onions, cut into 1-inch (2.5-cm) sections, white and green parts separated	½ teaspoon salt, 1 tablespoon thin soy sauce	8–10 minutes, reducing heat and adding wok lid for second half of time
1½ lb (700 g) white cabbage, cut into pieces, the stalk cooked first for 2 minutes	3 tablespoons	3 slices peeled fresh ginger root; 2–3 spring onions, cut into 1-inch (2.5-cm) sections, white and green parts separated	½ teaspoon salt, 2 teaspoons thin soy sauce	6–10 minutes, reducing heat and adding wok lid for second half of time
1 large head Cos or Iceberg lettuce, broken into large pieces	3 tablespoons	3 slices peeled fresh ginger root; 2–3 spring onions, cut into 1-inch (2.5-cm) sections, white and green parts separated	½ teaspoon salt, 1 tablespoon oyster sauce	2–3 minutes

Vegetable	Vegetable oil	Condiments	Seasoning	Stir-frying time
1 head celery, sliced diagonally at ¼-inch (6-mm) intervals	2½–3 tablespoons	3 slices peeled fresh ginger root; 2–3 spring onions, cut into 1-inch (2.5-cm) sections, white and green parts separated	½–¾ teaspoon salt	1–1½ minutes
1 long cucumber, cut as for French fries	3 tablespoons	3 slices peeled fresh ginger root; 2–3 spring onions, cut into 1-inch (2.5-cm) sections, white and green parts separated	½ teaspoon salt	2–3 minutes
1 lb (450 g) spinach, blanched for 20 seconds and drained	5 tablespoons	4–5 cloves garlic, peeled and finely chopped	½–¾ teaspoon salt	6–7 minutes
8 oz (250 g) fresh mushrooms, cut into slices	2 tablespoons	2–3 spring onions, cut into 1-inch (2.5-cm) sections, white and green parts separated	¼–⅓ teaspoon salt	2–4 minutes

Stir-fried Whole Scallops

12 fresh sea scallops, cleaned
1½ teaspoons salt
2 tablespoons vegetable oil
4 oz (100 g) mange-tout, *trimmed*
oil for deep-frying
2–3 cloves garlic, peeled and cut
  diagonally into slices
3–4 thin slices fresh ginger root, peeled
2 spring onions, cut into 2-inch (5-cm)
  sections, white and green parts
  separated
1 tablespoon Shaoxing wine or
  medium dry sherry

FOR THE SAUCE mix together
1 teaspoon potato flour or 1⅓
  teaspoons cornflour
5–6 tablespoons well-seasoned
  ham bone or chicken stock

FOR THE DIPS
oyster sauce (see page 13)
chilli sauce

Sea scallops, or Coquilles Saint-Jacques, are a luxurious treat when in season. Their fibrous white meat, if not properly cooked, however, can become a rubbery mass hateful to the palate. It is therefore worth your while to pay close attention to the instructions detailed in this recipe if you wish to achieve the delicate and special dish it should be.

1. Separate the coral from the white meat of each scallop. Remove the hard cartilage which can be put into the stockpot. Remove and discard the black vein and any membrane around the white meat. Pat dry both corals and white pieces. Using a small pointed knife, insert a noughts and crosses pattern into the white meat from both ends. This makes for an even and fast distribution of heat when they are cooking.
2. Half-fill the wok with boiling water, add 1 teaspoon of the salt and 1 tablespoon of the oil. Add the *mange-tout*. As soon as the water returns to a fierce rolling boil, pour into a colander and quickly refresh the *mange-tout* under cold running water. Drain thoroughly. This process retains the crispness and the vivid colour of the *mange-tout*, giving them a sheen as well. Dry the wok.
3. Fill the wok with about 1½ pints (850 ml, 4 cups) oil and heat over a moderate heat to a temperature of 200–225°F (100–110°C), or until the oil is only temperately hot. Add the corals and steep for about 30 seconds. Add the white meat and steep together for another 1–1½ minutes, separating with a long pair of chopsticks or wooden spoon. Lift with a large hand strainer or perforated spoon on to a dish. Separate the corals from the white meat.
4. Carefully empty all but about 1–2 tablespoons of the oil into a container and save for other use. Reheat the oil until hot. Add the garlic, let sizzle and take on colour, add the ginger and white spring onion and stir several times to release their aroma. Add the corals, turn and

toss with the wok scoop or metal spatula about half a dozen times, then add the white meat. Lowering the heat so as not to harden the white meat, continue to turn and toss for 20–30 seconds. Season with ¼ teaspoon salt. Splash the wine or sherry around the side of the wok, continuing to turn and toss until the sizzling subsides. Remove to a dish and keep warm nearby.

5. Turn the heat up to high and add the remaining 1 tablespoon oil to the wok. Add the *mange-tout* and stir rapidly over medium heat until very hot. Season with about ¼ teaspoon salt or to taste. Remove them to the sides and pour the well-stirred sauce into the centre, stirring as it thickens. Return the scallop coral and white to the wok, add the green spring onion and stir to mix. Remove to a serving dish. The white meat is tender and barely cooked while the corals are cooked just to a turn.

6. Serve immediately. The oyster sauce at the table is to be used to enhance the taste, while the chilli sauce is used optionally.

Prawns in Black Bean Sauce

1 lb (450 g) medium-sized fresh or
frozen raw prawns in the shell but
without heads, shelled and deveined
(see page 13)
4 tablespoons vegetable oil
1 large green pepper, seeded and
roughly chopped
4–5 cloves garlic, peeled and finely
chopped
2 fresh red chillies, seeded and cut into
small rounds (optional)
3 spring onions, cut into 1-inch
(2.5-cm) sections, white and green
parts separated
2 tablespoons preserved black beans
(see page 13), mashed with 1–2
teaspoons water and ½ teaspoon
sugar
½ teaspoon potato flour or ¾ teaspoon
cornflour dissolved in 3 tablespoons
water or chicken stock

FOR THE MARINADE
½ teaspoon salt
1 teaspoon cornflour
1 tablespoon egg white

In preparing this dish, the goal is to make the texture of
the prawns crisp. Thus, both ginger and alcohol are to
be avoided.

1. Marinate the prawns. Pat the prawns dry, then add
the salt, cornflour and egg white and stir in the same
direction to coat. Leave to stand, covered, in the refrigerator for 1–2 hours. (It can also be left overnight.) This
process gives the prawns the crisp texture looked for
when cooked.
2. Heat the wok over a medium heat until hot. Add 1
tablespoon of the oil and swirl it around. Add the green
pepper and stir for about 2 minutes. Remove on to a
dish and keep nearby. Wipe dry the wok.
3. Reheat over a high heat until smoke rises. Add the
remaining 3 tablespoons oil and swirl it around several
times. Add the garlic, let sizzle, then the chilli and white
spring onion and stir a few times. Add the mashed black
beans, stirring to mix. Add the prawns and, going to the
bottom of the wok with the scoop or a metal spatula,
turn and toss for 30–60 seconds or until the prawns are
partially cooked, becoming pinkish. Lower the heat,
pour in the well-stirred dissolved potato flour or
cornflour, stirring as it thickens. Return the green
pepper to the wok and add the green spring onion,
continuing to stir to mix. The prawns should be cooked
to a turn by now. Remove to a serving plate and serve
immediately.

Beef with Mange-tout

8 oz (225 g) trimmed beef (fillet, rump
  or skirt), cut across the grain into
  rectangular slices about
  ¾ × 1½ inches (2 × 4 cm) and
  ⅕ inch (5 mm) thick
1 teaspoon salt
5 tablespoons vegetable oil
8–12 oz (225–350 g) mange-tout
2–3 large cloves garlic, peeled and cut
  diagonally into thin slices
3–4 thin slices fresh ginger root, peeled
3–4 spring onions, cut into 1-inch
  (2.5-cm) sections, white and green
  parts separated
1 tablespoon Shaoxing wine or
  medium dry sherry

FOR THE MARINADE
¼ teaspoon salt
¼ teaspoon sugar
2–3 teaspoons thick soy sauce
6–8 turns black pepper mill
1 teaspoon Shaoxing wine or medium
  dry sherry
1 teaspoon potato flour or 1⅓
  teaspoons cornflour
1 tablespoon water
1 teaspoon sesame oil

FOR THE SAUCE mix together
½ teaspoon potato flour or ¾ teaspoon
  cornflour
3 tablespoons water and
1½ tablespoons oyster sauce or 1
  tablespoon thick soy sauce

This recipe can be used as a guideline for stir-fried beef with other green vegetables. The *mange-tout* can be substituted by Iceberg or Cos lettuce, broccoli, green beans or even spinach. When using broccoli or green beans, however, blanch them (step 2) longer (2–4 minutes) until they are tender yet still crisp.

1. Marinate the beef. Add the salt, sugar, soy sauce, pepper, wine or sherry and potato flour or cornflour to the beef and stir in the same direction to coat. Add the water, stirring until completely absorbed. Leave to stand in the refrigerator for 15–30 minutes. Blend in the oil.
2. Half-fill the wok with water and bring to the boil. Add the salt and 1 tablespoon of the oil. Plunge in the *mange-tout* and return to a rolling boil. Pour into a colander and refresh the *mange-tout* under cold running water. Drain.
3. Reheat the wok over a high heat until smoke rises. Add 3 tablespoons oil and swirl it around several times. Add the garlic, let sizzle, then add the ginger and the white spring onion and stir to release their aroma. Add the beef and, sliding the wok scoop or a metal spatula to the bottom of the wok, turn and toss for about 30 seconds or until partially cooked. Splash the wine or sherry around the side of the wok, continuing to stir. When the sizzling subsides, remove the beef, still underdone, to a dish and keep warm.
4. Add the remaining 1 tablespoon oil to the wok and swirl it around. Return the *mange-tout* to the wok and turn and toss over a moderate heat until thoroughly hot, taking care not to burn them. Push them to the sides of the wok, pour the well-stirred sauce into the centre, and stir as it thickens. Return the beef to the sauce, stirring to mix. Add the green spring onion, stir in the *mange-tout* from the sides. Remove to a serving plate and serve immediately.

Beef with Pineapple

4 large rounds of fresh pineapple,
 ½ inch (1 cm) thick, cored and cut
 into chunks
small pinch salt
about 2 teaspoons sugar
1 lb (450 g) rump steak or skirt,
 trimmed and cut across the grain
 into rectangular slices about
 ¾ × 1½ inches (2 × 4 cm) and
 ⅕ inch (5 mm) thick
5½ tablespoons vegetable oil
2 large cloves garlic, peeled and cut
 diagonally into thin slices
3 spring onions, cut into 1-inch
 (2.5-cm) sections, white and green
 parts separated
8 thin slices peeled fresh ginger root,
 cut into very fine silky strips
1 tablespoon Shaoxing wine or
 medium dry sherry
½ teaspoon potato flour or ¾ teaspoon
 cornflour dissolved in 2 tablespoons
 water

FOR THE MARINADE
½ teaspoon salt
¼ teaspoon sugar
1 tablespoon thick soy sauce
8 turns black pepper mill
2 teaspoons Shaoxing wine or medium
 dry sherry
1¼ teaspoons potato flour or 1½
 teaspoons cornflour
1–2 tablespoons water
1 teaspoon sesame oil

Because of the warm climate in South China, tropical fruits abound, and it is not unusual to combine fruit with meat or poultry. Pineapples and mangoes are favourites with beef, affecting an appetizingly sweet and sour taste in the dish.

1. Taste the pineapple for acidity, then add the salt and sugar accordingly. Mix well and leave to stand for 30 minutes or longer.
2. Marinate the beef. Add the salt, sugar, soy sauce, pepper, wine or sherry and potato flour or cornflour to the beef and stir in the same direction to coat. Add the water, 1 tablespoonful at a time, stirring until completely absorbed before adding another spoonful. Leave to stand in the refrigerator for 15–20 minutes. Blend in the oil.
3. Heat the wok over a high heat until smoke rises. Add 4 tablespoons of the oil and swirl it around several times. Add the garlic, let sizzle, then the white spring onion and half of the ginger and stir to release their aroma. Add the beef and, sliding the wok scoop or a metal spatula to the bottom of the wok, turn and toss for about 30 seconds or until the beef is partially cooked. Splash the wine or sherry around the side of the wok. When the sizzling subsides, remove the beef, still underdone, to a dish and keep warm nearby.
4. Add the remaining 1½ tablespoons oil to the wok and swirl it around over a high heat. Add the remaining ginger, stir a few times then add the pineapple. Stir until piping hot, adjusting the heat to medium. Push the pineapple to the edges and pour the well-stirred dissolved potato flour or cornflour into the centre of the wok, continuing to stir as it thickens. Return the beef to the wok, add the green spring onion and stir to mix until thoroughly hot again. Remove on to a serving dish and serve immediately.

Lambs' Kidney in Marsala Sauce

Serves 2 as a main course

6 lambs' kidneys
4 tablespoons vegetable oil
*3 large cloves garlic, peeled and cut
    diagonally into thin slices*
2–2½ tablespoons Marsala wine
*1 teaspoon cornflour dissolved in 3
    tablespoons water*
1 oz (25 g) almond flakes

FOR THE MARINADE
1 teaspoon salt
black pepper to taste
*2 teaspoons fresh ginger juice (see page
    15)*
1 tablespoon sesame oil

Lambs' kidney, subtle in taste and texture, can easily become rubbery if it is overcooked. By stir-frying it, however, you can cook it to a turn, or even have it slightly underdone. In this recipe, the interaction between the salt, ginger juice, sesame oil and Marsala wine produces a scrumptious result.

1. Carefully remove the white fatty lumps and membranes of the kidneys. Cut each crossways into about 6 pieces, removing any remaining white membranes. Put into a bowl.
2. Marinate the kidney. Add the salt, pepper and ginger juice to the kidney and mix well. Leave to stand for about 30 minutes. Blend in the oil.
3. Heat the wok over a high heat until smoke rises. Add the oil and swirl it around several times. Add the garlic, let sizzle and take on colour, then add the kidney. Sliding the wok scoop or a metal spatula to the bottom of the wok, flip and turn continuously for 1½ minutes until the pieces begin to turn opaque. Splash in the Marsala wine around the side of the wok and, as it sizzles, continue to stir for another 1½ minutes. Lower the heat to medium, pour in the well-stirred dissolved cornflour and stir as it thickens. Continue to cook for another 30–60 seconds then remove to a serving dish. The kidney is slightly underdone and juicy. Sprinkle with the almond flakes and serve.

VARIATION: *Veal Kidney in Marsala Sauce*

Use a veal kidney about 1–1¼ lb (450–550 g), cut crossways into thin slices about ¼ inch (6 mm) thick, then proceed as above.

Stir-fried Pork with Leek

1 lb (450 g) lean pork, cut into
    rectangular pieces about
    ¾ × 2 inches (2 × 5 cm) and
    ⅛ inch (3 mm) thick
6 tablespoons vegetable oil
1 lb (450 g) leeks, trimmed, cut into
    ¾-inch (2-cm) rounds and
    separated, washed thoroughly
salt
3 large cloves garlic, peeled and sliced
    diagonally into thin pieces
1 tablespoon Shaoxing wine or
    medium dry sherry

FOR THE MARINADE
⅓ teaspoon salt
¼ teaspoon sugar
1 tablespoon thin soy sauce
8 turns white pepper mill
2 teaspoons Shaoxing wine or medium
    dry sherry
1 teaspoon potato flour or 1⅓
    teaspoons cornflour
1 tablespoon water
1 tablespoon vegetable oil
1 teaspoon sesame oil

FOR THE SAUCE mix together
¾ teaspoon potato flour or 1 teaspoon
    cornflour
5 tablespoons water
1–2 tablespoons oyster sauce or 2–3
    teaspoons thick soy sauce

Leeks cut up and separated into single rings can be very tender when stir-fried. When they are then combined with pork, they make a delicious dish together.

1. Marinate the pork. Add the salt, sugar, soy sauce, pepper, wine or sherry and potato flour or cornflour to the pork and stir to coat. Add the water and stir until it is absorbed. Leave to stand for about 20 minutes, then blend in the oils.
2. Heat the wok over a high heat until smoke rises. Add 2 tablespoons oil and swirl it around. Add the leeks, stir for about 1 minute, lowering the heat to medium so as not to burn them. Season with about ¼–½ teaspoon salt, then cover and cook in their own juice for about 2 minutes. Stir thoroughly again and continue to cook, covered, for another 2–3 minutes until the leeks are tender. Remove on to a plate and keep warm nearby. Wipe dry the wok.
3. Reheat the wok over a high heat until smoke rises. Add the remaining 4 tablespoons oil and swirl it around. Add the garlic, let sizzle and take on colour. Add the pork and, going to the bottom of the wok with the wok scoop or metal spatula, toss and turn for about 1 minute or until the pork is partially cooked. Splash in the wine or sherry around the side of the wok, continuing to stir as it sizzles. Lower the heat, push the pork to the sloping side and pour the well-stirred sauce into the centre, stirring as it thickens. Fold in the pork, which should be cooked by now, and return the leek, stirring to mix. Remove to a serving plate and serve immediately.

Shredded Pork with Cucumber

12 oz (350 g) lean pork, pat dried and
   cut into strips about 2 inches (5 cm)
   long and ⅕ inch (5 mm) thick
4½ tablespoons vegetable oil
2–3 thin slices fresh ginger root, peeled
1 cucumber, about 12 oz–1 lb
   (350–450 g), cut as for French fries
½ teaspoon salt
3 fresh green chillies, seeded or
   unseeded, cut into small rounds
   (optional)
2–3 large cloves garlic, peeled and cut
   into strips
3–4 large spring onions, cut into
   2-inch (5-cm) sections, white and
   green parts separated
1 tablespoon Shaoxing wine or
   medium dry sherry

FOR THE MARINADE
½ teaspoon salt
¼ teaspoon sugar
2 teaspoons thin soy sauce
6–8 turns white pepper mill
2 teaspoons Shaoxing wine or medium
   dry sherry
1 teaspoon potato flour or 1⅓
   teaspoons cornflour
1 teaspoon sesame oil
2 teaspoons vegetable oil

FOR THE SAUCE mix together
¾ teaspoon potato flour or 1 teaspoon
   cornflour
1½ teaspoons thick soy sauce
4 tablespoons water

By using or by not using the spicy hot green chillies, this family dish can suit all palates. Either way, it is appetizing.

1. Marinate the pork: Add the salt, sugar, soy sauce, pepper, wine or sherry, potato flour or cornflour to the pork and stir to coat well. Leave to stand for 15–20 minutes. Blend in the oils.
2. Heat the wok over a high heat until smoke rises. Add 1½ tablespoons of the oil and swirl it around. Add the ginger, let sizzle, then add the cucumber. Season with the salt and stir continuously for about 1½ minutes or until very hot. Remove on to a plate and keep warm nearby. Wipe dry the wok.
3. Reheat wok over a high heat until smoke rises. Add the remaining 3 tablespoons oil and swirl it around several times. Add the chilli, if used, and stir a couple of times. Add the garlic, let sizzle, and then add the white spring onion and stir a few times to release the aroma. Add the pork and, going to the bottom of the wok with the wok scoop or a metal spatula, flip and toss continuously for about 1 minute or until the pork is whitish in colour. Splash in the wine or sherry around the side of the wok, continuing to stir. When the sizzling dies down, add the well-stirred sauce, stirring as it thickens. Return the cucumber to the wok and add the green spring onion. Stir to mix until very hot again. Remove to a serving plate and serve immediately.

Chicken in Black Bean Sauce

1 chicken, 2¼–2½ lb (1–1.1 kg),
  cleaned, chopped through skin and
  bones into 1-inch (2.5-cm) pieces
4 tablespoons vegetable oil
1 medium-sized green pepper, seeded
  and roughly chopped
salt to taste
15–20 cloves garlic, peeled and left
  whole
4 large spring onions, cut into 2-inch
  (5-cm) sections, white and green
  parts separated
3–3½ tablespoons preserved black
  beans, three-quarters mashed and
  one-quarter left whole (see page 13)
1 tablespoon Shaoxing wine or
  medium dry sherry
1 teaspoon potato flour or 1⅓
  teaspoons cornflour dissolved in 4
  tablespoons water

FOR THE MARINADE
½ teaspoon salt
½ teaspoon sugar
1 tablespoon thin soy sauce
8 turns black pepper mill
2 teaspoons Shaoxing wine or medium
  dry sherry

The Chinese love to suck chicken bones, and they often chop the bird into fairly small pieces either before or after cooking it. When stir-fried in black beans and lots of garlic, the chicken pieces are scrumptious.

1. Marinate the chicken. Add the salt, sugar, soy sauce, pepper and wine or sherry to the chicken and mix thoroughly. Leave to stand for about 30 minutes. Separate the white breast pieces from the rest.
2. Heat the wok over a high heat until smoke rises. Add ½ tablespoon of the oil and swirl it around. Add the green pepper, season with a pinch of salt and stir for about 1 minute over medium heat. Remove and keep nearby.
3. Reheat the wok over a high heat until smoke rises. Add the remaining 3½ tablespoons oil and swirl it around several times. Add the garlic, fry for about 30 seconds or until it takes on colour. Add the white spring onion, stir a few times, then add the black beans and stir together to release their aroma. Add the chicken, except for the breast pieces, and, going to the bottom of the wok with the wok scoop or a metal spatula, turn and toss vigorously for about 2 minutes. Add the breast pieces and continue to turn and toss for another minute. Splash the wine or sherry around the sides of the wok, stirring all the time. When the sizzling subsides, lower the heat to medium, put on the wok lid and continue to cook for about 4 minutes. Remove the lid, stir, turning over the pieces which should have oozed out juices. Taste the dark meat for readiness, then continue to cook, covered, for another 3–5 minutes or until just cooked to a turn.
4. Remove the lid, return the green pepper to the wok and stir together with the chicken until hot. Pour in the well-stirred dissolved potato flour or cornflour, stirring as it thickens. Add the green spring onion, mix and remove to a serving dish and serve immediately.

Chicken with Celery and Cashew Nuts

12 oz (350 g) skinned and boned
  chicken breast, cut into slices about
  1/3 inch (8 mm) thick
5 tablespoons vegetable oil
4 sticks celery, cut diagonally into
  slices about 1/8 inch (3 mm) thick
salt
2–3 large cloves garlic, peeled and
  sliced diagonally
3 spring onions, cut into 1-inch
  (2.5-cm) sections, white and green
  parts separated
1 tablespoon Shaoxing wine or
  medium dry sherry
2–3 oz (50–75 g) roasted cashew nuts

FOR THE MARINADE
1/3 teaspoon salt
1/4 teaspoon sugar
2 teaspoons thin soy sauce
8 turns white pepper mill
2 teaspoons Shaoxing wine or medium
  dry sherry
1 teaspoon cornflour
1 tablespoon egg white
2 teaspoons vegetable oil
1 teaspoon sesame oil

FOR THE SAUCE mix together
1 teaspoon potato flour or 1 1/3
  teaspoons cornflour
5 tablespoons water
1 tablespoon oyster sauce or 2
  teaspoons thick soy sauce

This is a combination that greatly pleases the Western palate. The Chinese also like it but don't necessarily always include the cashew nuts. The crunchiness of the celery and the nuts provides contrast to the tenderness of the chicken. Texture is the essence of Chinese cooking.

1. Marinate the chicken. Add the salt, sugar, soy sauce, pepper and wine or sherry to the chicken and mix to coat. Sprinkle with the cornflour, add the egg white and stir to coat well. Leave to stand for about 15–20 minutes. Blend in the oils.
2. Heat the wok over a high heat until smoke rises. Add 1 tablespoon of the oil and swirl it around. Add the celery and stir rapidly for 1 minute, seasoning with a pinch of salt. The celery should be crunchy even though cooked. Remove and keep warm nearby. Wipe dry the wok.
3. Reheat over a high heat until smoke rises. Add the remaining 4 tablespoons of oil and swirl it around. Add the garlic, let sizzle, then add the white spring onion and stir a few times to release their aroma. Add the chicken and, going to the bottom of the wok with the scoop or metal spatula, flip and turn for 30–60 seconds or until the chicken is becoming opaque. Splash in the wine or sherry around the side of the wok, continuing to stir as it sizzles. Add the well-stirred sauce and continue to stir until it thickens. Return the celery to the wok, add the nuts and the green spring onion and stir to mix. Remove to a serving plate and serve immediately.

Slippery Egg and Shrimps

6 large eggs
⅓–½ teaspoon salt
1 teaspoon sesame oil
3 spring onions, cut into small
    rounds, green and white parts
    separated
about 8 fl oz (225 ml) vegetable oil
8 oz (225 g) peeled cooked frozen
    shrimps, thoroughly defrosted and
    patted dry

This recipe sets out the basic technique of Chinese scrambled egg, or 'slippery egg' in Chinese. The shrimps can be omitted or substituted by diced ham or cooked crab meat. In China, uncooked shrimps would be marinated in salt, egg white and cornflour, chilled for several hours then lightly cooked before they are added to the beaten egg. But in the West, frozen cooked rather than raw shrimps are much more easily available, so I have adapted the recipe to use cooked shrimps.

1. Beat the eggs until homogenized. Add the salt, sesame oil and green spring onion and mix well.
2. Heat the wok over a high heat until smoke rises. Add 1 tablespoon of the oil and swirl it around. Add the white spring onion and stir a few times to release its aroma. Remove the wok from the heat, add the shrimps and stir to mix. Return the wok over a low heat and stir the shrimps for another 20–30 seconds or until they are just warm. (As they are already cooked, reheating over a high heat would make them rubbery.) Remove and mix into the beaten egg. Wash and dry the wok.
3. Reheat the wok over a high heat until smoke rises. Pour in about 6 fl oz (175 ml, ¾ cup) oil, swirl it around reaching over half-way up the slope of the wok, then pour back into a container for other use. This prevents the egg from sticking to the wok when it is cooked.
4. Add 4 tablespoons of the oil and swirl it around several times. Lower the heat to medium. Pour in the egg mixture and, going to the bottom of the wok with the wok scoop or a metal spatula, fold over the egg as soon as it is set, giving room for the still runny egg to be cooked. At the same time, stream 1 tablespoon oil around the side of the wok to make the egg that much more slippery in texture. Serve immediately.

Note: this dish not only goes well with rice but is equally delicious served on toast.

Stir-fried Milk

groundnut or vegetable oil
6 oz (175 g) fresh white mushrooms,
  roughly chopped
salt
1½ oz (40 g) rice sticks, broken into
  2½-inch (6.5-cm) lengths
3 tabl. spoons cornflour
1 pint (568 ml, 2½ cups) milk, creamy
  best
6 large egg whites, about 8 oz (225 g)
4 oz (100 g) cooked crabmeat or peeled
  shrimps
white pepper to taste
1–2 oz (25–50 g) ham, minced

This strange-sounding dish originated sometime during the early part of the 20th century in Daliang, a county near Canton renowned for the ingenuity of its chefs who exerted great influence on Cantonese cooking.

1. Heat the wok over a high heat until smoke rises. Add 1 tablespoon of the oil and swirl it around. Add the mushroom, season with ¼ teaspoon salt and stir rapidly for about 1½–2 minutes until cooked. Put into a sieve to drain. Wash and dry the wok.
2. Half-fill the wok with oil and heat to 350°F (180°C), or until 1 rice stick rises to the surface instantly. Add the rice sticks which will sink to the bottom then rise to the surface, expanding into a snow-white woven mass. Gently press them down once with a large hand strainer or perforated disc to make sure that they are thoroughly deep-fried. Remove at once to drain on kitchen paper then transfer to line a large serving plate. Pour the oil into a container for other use. Wash and dry the wok.
3. Dissolve the cornflour in 3–4 tablespoons of the milk.
4. Gently break up the gel of the egg whites. Stir in the remaining milk, crabmeat and mushroom. Season with ½–¾ teaspoon salt and white pepper to taste and add the well-stirred dissolved cornflour.
5. Reheat the wok over a high heat until smoke rises. Add 7 tablespoons clean and unused oil and swirl it to half-way up the wok. Give the milk mixture one more stir and pour into the wok. Lower the heat and, using the back of the wok scoop, move the liquid mixture away from the sides, towards the centre. As it slowly solidifies, let the still runny mixture go to the sides and bottom to be cooked, taking care that it does not stick. As soon as it has all set, remove from the heat and scoop on to the rice sticks. Sprinkle with ham and serve.

Note: take care not to overcook the milk or water will start oozing out.

Family Bean Curd

6 oz (175 g) minced beef
4 cakes firm bean curd, each about
    2½ inches (6.5 cm) square and
    1¼ inches (3 cm) thick
3 tablespoons vegetable oil
2 cloves garlic, peeled and finely
    chopped
3 spring onions, cut into small
    rounds, white and green parts
    separated
1 tablespoon Shaoxing wine or
    medium dry sherry
5 fl oz (150 ml) chicken or beef stock
1 teaspoon potato flour or 1⅓
    teaspoons cornflour dissolved in 1
    tablespoon water
1–2 teaspoons sesame oil

FOR THE MARINADE
¾ teaspoon salt
¼ teaspoon sugar
1 tablespoon thick soy sauce
6 turns black pepper mill
1 teaspoon Shaoxing wine or medium
    dry sherry
1 teaspoon potato flour or 1⅓
    teaspoons cornflour
1 tablespoon water

So called when the bean curd, cooked with a small amount of meat, either pork or beef, is seasoned harmoniously with soy sauce but without any spicy hot condiments such as chilli so that everybody in the family, old and young, with or without a highly developed palate, can eat it.

1. Marinate the beef. Add the salt, sugar, soy sauce, pepper, wine or sherry and potato flour or cornflour to the beef and stir in the same direction until well coated. Add the water and stir again until absorbed. Leave to stand for 15–20 minutes.
2. Steep the bean curds in hot water for about 15 minutes. Drain, handling with care. Put on either a tea towel or kitchen paper to absorb all the excess water. Cut each bean curd cake into 32 cubes: quarter lengthways and crossways, then halve each piece.
3. Heat the wok over a high heat until smoke rises. Add the oil and swirl it around. Add the garlic, then the white spring onion and stir several times. Add the beef and, going to the bottom of the wok with the wok scoop or metal spatula, flip and toss for about 1 minute. Splash in the wine or sherry around the side of the wok, stirring continuously. When the sizzling subsides, pour in the stock, lower the heat and let the beef simmer in the stock for 5–10 minutes. Stir in the dissolved potato flour or cornflour. (This sauce can be made several hours ahead and left in the wok.)
4. Add the bean curd to the meat sauce. Gently turn and fold the mixture over a medium heat until the bean curd is piping hot. Sprinkle on the green spring onion. Scoop on to a serving dish. Sprinkle on the sesame oil and serve hot.

West Lake Beef Soup (Soups: page 20).

**Steamed Siu Mai
(Steaming: page 25).**

Steamed Grey Mullet (Steaming: page 26).

Bean Curd with Pork (Sautéing: page 66)
with Steamed Rice (page 31) and Sauté Pouch Egg (page 72)

Shrimp Stir-fried Rice

6 loose cups cooked rice (see Steamed
   Rice, page 31)
8 oz (225 g) frozen petits pois
8 oz (225 g) cooked shrimps
5 tablespoons vegetable oil
2 cloves garlic, peeled and finely
   chopped
1 teaspoon salt
6 spring onions, cut into small
   rounds, white and green parts
   separated
1 very large or 2 small eggs, lightly
   beaten
thin or thick soy sauce

In China one would always use raw shrimps, but as in this country shrimps and prawns are more commonly sold pre-cooked I have used cooked shrimps in this recipe. Just make sure that you simply heat them through and don't cook them too rapidly. Overcooked shrimps lose their delicate and juicy texture.

1. Leave the cooked rice, covered, for 4–5 hours or overnight. Loosen the grains, breaking up lumps just before use.
2. Blanch the *petits pois* in a pot of salted water for 2–3 minutes. Drain well. If frozen cooked shrimps are used, defrost and then pat dry well.
3. Heat the wok over a high heat until smoke rises. Add 1½ tablespoons of the oil and swirl it around. Add the garlic which will sizzle, taking on colour. Add the shrimps, season with ½ teaspoon of salt and stir rapidly for 30–60 seconds until hot in order to incorporate the oil and fragrance. Do not overcook them lest they become tough and chewy. Remove to a dish and keep warm nearby. Wipe dry the wok.
4. Reheat the wok over a high heat until smoke rises. Add the remaining 3½ tablespoons oil and swirl it around. Add the white spring onion and stir a few times. Pour in the egg and let it set at the bottom for a few seconds while the surface is still runny. Add the well-loosened rice and, going to the bottom of the wok with the wok scoop or metal spatula, flip and turn rapidly for 2–3 minutes or until the rice is thoroughly hot. Add the remaining ½ teaspoon salt and the *petits pois*, continuing to stir until piping hot again. Return the shrimps to the wok, add the green spring onion and stir to mix. Transfer to a serving bowl or dish and serve immediately. Thin or thick soy sauce can be added at the table to suit individual taste.

Mixed Fried Rice

6 tablespoons vegetable oil

4 oz (100 g) canned bamboo shoots, diced

4 oz (100 g) cucumber, diced

4 oz (100 g) frozen petits pois, blanched in salted water for 3 minutes, drained

4–6 spring onions, cut into small rounds, white and green parts separated

2 eggs, lightly beaten with ¼ teaspoon salt

6 loose cups cooked rice (see page 31), grains loosened and separated

½ teaspoon salt

8 oz (225 g) grilled or fried streaky bacon, diced

8 oz (225 g) roast chicken, diced

1 tablespoon thin soy sauce, or to taste

A delicious fried rice dish fit for guests and family as the main course for 4–5 people, to be washed down with beer, cider or white wine. You can vary the ingredients and use up left-overs as long as you keep the basics – rice, spring onion and egg.

1. Heat the wok over a high heat until smoke rises. Add 2 tablespoons of the oil and swirl it around. Add the bamboo shoots and cucumber. Stir and turn rapidly for 1–2 minutes until piping hot. Remove to a dish and mix in the *petits pois*. Wash and dry the wok.

2. Reheat the wok over a high heat until smoke rises. Add the remaining 4 tablespoons oil and swirl it around several times. Add the white spring onion and stir to release its aroma. Pour in the egg and leave for a few seconds to set partially. Add the rice. (The egg is still half runny and will moisten the rice.) Sliding the wok scoop or a metal spatula to the bottom of the wok, flip and turn rapidly until the rice is hot. Season with the salt and add the bacon and chicken, continuing to stir until the mixture is hot again. Add the bamboo shoots mixture and stir again until hot. Add the soy sauce and green spring onion. Stir to mix, test for taste, then scoop into a large serving bowl. Serve immediately.

French Beans with Garlic

boiling water
salt
5 tablespoons vegetable oil
1 lb (450 g) French beans, trimmed
6 large cloves garlic, peeled and finely
    chopped
2 teaspoons thin soy sauce

If it seems a lot of garlic for a pound of beans, do not be alarmed, for the Chinese way of frying the garlic in hot oil releases its aroma which is then transmitted to the beans. The result is a special 'wok fragrance' in the beans without the unpleasant odour associated with garlic. The same principle can be applied to preparing runner beans, although they should be blanched for a little longer.

1. Half-fill the wok with boiling water and keep it boiling. Add 1 teaspoon salt and 1½ tablespoons of oil, which will preserve the vivid colour of the beans when cooked. Add the beans and blanch for 2–4 minutes depending on size; they should still have a bite to them. Pour into a colander and immediately rinse thoroughly under cold running water in order to retain their crisp texture. Drain.
2. Dry the wok. Reheat over a high heat until smoke rises. Add the remaining oil and swirl it around. Add the garlic, stir as it sizzles and takes on colour. Add the beans and, going to the bottom of the wok with the wok scoop, flip and turn rapidly for 1–2 minutes or until the beans are thoroughly hot. Adjust the heat if necessary so that the beans do not burn. Add the soy sauce, stir to mix, then remove to a serving plate and serve hot.

Stir-fried Courgettes

1 lb (450 g) medium-sized courgettes
about 1¼ teaspoons salt
3 tablespoons vegetable oil
4 thin slices fresh ginger root, peeled
2–3 spring onions, cut into 1-inch
    (2.5-cm) sections, white and green
    parts separated
1–2 teaspoons thin soy sauce

Courgette, or zucchini, is not a Chinese vegetable, but if sliced thinly can be adapted to wok stir-frying most successfully. In fact, cooked this way, not only will this vegetable's vivid colour be retained but a crisp texture will be introduced. To achieve this effect, however, it is important to draw out the water beforehand, thereby getting rid of its slightly bitter taste as well as preventing it from going soggy in a pool of liquid when cooked.

1. Wash the courgettes, cut and discard the tops and ends. Slice crossways into thin slivers no more than ¹⁄₁₀ inch (2 mm) thick. Put into a large bowl. Sprinkle with the salt and mix thoroughly. Leave to stand for about 20 minutes or until water has been drawn out. Drain but leave damp.
2. Heat the wok over a high heat until smoke rises. Add the oil and swirl it around. Add the ginger then the white spring onion and let sizzle for a few seconds to release their aroma. Add the courgette and, sliding the wok scoop to the bottom of the wok, flip and turn for about 1 minute. Lower the heat to medium and continue to turn and toss for about 3 minutes or until the courgette is tender yet still has a bite to it. Test for taste then add the soy sauce. Add the green spring onion, stir and remove to a serving plate. Serve immediately.

Chinese Broccoli with Ginger Juice

1 lb (450 g) Chinese broccoli, washed and trimmed
salt
4 tablespoons vegetable oil
1–1½ inches (2.5–4 cm) fresh ginger root, peeled and finely chopped
1 tablespoon Shaoxing wine or medium dry sherry
2 tablespoons oyster sauce (see page 13)

Compared to ordinary broccoli, Chinese broccoli is more subtle in taste, reminiscent of asparagus. This subtle taste is further enhanced by the infusion of the mixture of ginger juice and Shaoxing wine. If Chinese broccoli is not available, ordinary broccoli can be used instead, and its taste will also benefit from the wine and ginger juice.

1. Break up the leafy parts of the broccoli and cut the stalks diagonally at ½-inch (1-cm) intervals. Leave the florets whole.
2. Bring a large pan of water to the boil, add 1 teaspoon salt and 1 tablespoon oil. Add the broccoli, return to the boil, then continue to boil for 2 minutes. The broccoli will still be very crunchy. Pour into a colander and drain.
3. Put the ginger, in several batches, into a garlic press, add 2 drops of water each time and squeeze the juice into a small bowl, scraping the minced ginger found on the surface of the press as well. Discard the pulp inside. Add the wine or sherry to the juice.
4. Heat the wok over a high heat until smoke rises. Add the remaining oil and swirl it around. Tip in the drained broccoli and stir to mix with the oil in the wok. Pour in the ginger juice with wine or sherry and sprinkle on a pinch of salt. Sliding the wok scoop or metal spatula to the bottom of the wok, flip and turn to allow the ginger juice and wine to be absorbed. Lower the heat to medium, add a little water (about 1 tablespoon) and cook, covered, for another minute. The broccoli should be crisp but not hard. Remove to a serving plate and lace over the oyster sauce. Serve hot.

Button Mushroom Vinaigrette

5 tablespoons vegetable oil
8–10 spring onions, cut into small
  rounds, white and green parts
  separated
1¼ lb (550 g) small button
  mushrooms, washed and trimmed
1 inch (2.5 cm) fresh ginger root,
  peeled and finely chopped
1 teaspoon salt
1 teaspoon sugar
3 tablespoons white wine vinegar

This vinaigrette mushroom, with its faint but refreshing ginger taste, is a winner as a first course or a side dish – especially for those who do not care for garlic in a vinaigrette sauce. It is usually served cold, but this dish is also very good hot. The sauce is rich and rather tart. When cold serve it with cold roast pork as a side dish.

1. Heat the wok over a high heat until smoke rises. Add the oil and swirl it around. Add the white spring onion and let it sizzle, releasing its aroma. Add the mushrooms and, sliding the wok scoop or a metal spatula to the bottom of the wok, turn and toss the mushrooms constantly for about 1 minute. Lower the heat to medium and continue to cook the mushrooms, which will gradually start oozing out water.
2. Put the ginger into a garlic press in about 3 batches, adding 2–3 drops of water each time, and squeeze the juice over the mushrooms. Add the minced ginger that was squeezed through the press as well, discarding the pulp inside. Add the salt, sugar and 2 tablespoons of the vinegar. Continue to cook the mushrooms for about 10 minutes over a fairly high heat, stirring from time to time. At the end of the cooking the sauce should be rich and tart. Add the remaining vinegar and the green spring onion and stir to mix.
3. Remove from the wok, allow to cool, then chill in the refrigerator for several hours or overnight. Serve cold.

Stir-fried Creamed Cauliflower

1 head cauliflower, 1½–2 lb
   (700–900 g)
about 3½ pints (2 litres, 9 cups) water
1 teaspoon salt
1 tablespoon vegetable oil
3–4 tablespoons rendered chicken fat or
   3–4 tablespoons vegetable oil
2–3 thin slices fresh ginger root, peeled
2–3 spring onions, cut into 2-inch
   (5-cm) sections, white and green
   parts separated

FOR THE SAUCE mix together
1 teaspoon potato flour or 1⅓
   teaspoons cornflour
6 fl oz (175 ml, ¾ cup) evaporated
   milk or single cream
¾–1 teaspoon salt

The Western influence in this 20th-century Chinese recipe is evident in the use of evaporated milk or cream. The Chinese version uses the traditional chicken fat which, when combined with the milk or cream, lends an added flavour to the vegetable.

1. Cut off and discard the outer hard stalks of the cauliflower. Cut the florets into uniform bite-sized pieces.
2. Fill the wok with water and bring to the boil. Add the salt and the oil. Plunge in the cauliflower and return to the boil. Continue to boil for 3–4 minutes or until the cauliflower is tender yet retains a bite to it. Pour into a colander and refresh under cold running water. Drain.
3. Heat the wok again over a high heat until smoke rises. Add the chicken fat or oil and swirl it around several times. Add the ginger, stir, then add the white spring onion and stir a few times to release its aroma. Return the cauliflower to the wok. Sliding the wok scoop or metal spatula to the bottom of the wok, turn and toss rapidly for about 1 minute or until piping hot, lowering the heat so as not to burn the cauliflower. Pour in the well-stirred sauce, continuing to stir until it thickens. Add the green spring onion. Remove to a serving dish and serve immediately.

Note: instead of cauliflower, Chinese celery cabbage (Chinese leaves) can be used.

Asparagus in Stock

1 lb (450 g) medium-sized asparagus,
cleaned
½ pint (300 ml, 1¼ cups)
concentrated but clear chicken or
ham stock
½ teaspoon salt
3 tablespoons vegetable oil
1½ teaspoons potato flour or 2
teaspoons cornflour dissolved in 1
tablespoon stock
4 thin slices fresh ginger root, peeled
2–3 spring onions, cut into 1-inch
(2.5-cm) sections, white and green
parts separated

A delicate vegetable like asparagus needs equally delicate culinary treatment. Steeping it in stock does just
that, enhancing its inherent sweetness while preserving
its pure taste.

1. Chop off and discard the hard end of each asparagus
stem. Halve the remainder. Split vertically half-way
down the thicker bottom half, ensuring more even cooking.
2. Pour the stock into the wok and bring it to the boil.
Add the salt and 1 tablespoon of the oil. Add the
asparagus, return to the boil, then continue to cook over
a gentle heat for about 3 minutes. Carefully transfer the
asparagus and stock to a bowl and leave the asparagus
to steep in the stock for about 1–2 hours. The asparagus
are tender yet still have a bite to them. Then lift them
out of the stock on to a dish.
3. Stir the dissolved potato flour or cornflour into half of
the stock, saving the remainder for other use.
4. Reheat the cleaned wok over a high heat until smoke
rises. Add the remaining 2 tablespoons oil and swirl it
around. Add the ginger, stir, then add the white spring
onion. Lowering the heat to medium, return the
asparagus to the wok and stir until thoroughly hot. Pour
in the well-stirred stock, continuing to stir as it thickens.
Mix in the green spring onion, then transfer to a serving
dish. Serve immediately.

Stir-fried Mixed Vegetables

boiling water
2 teaspoons salt
5 tablespoons vegetable oil
6 oz (175 g) green beans, trimmed and
  halved crossways if long
12 oz (350 g) white cabbage, cored and
  cut into fairly large pieces
6 oz (175 g) carrots, peeled and cut
  into both large and thin slices
4 oz (100 g) canned bamboo shoots, cut
  into both large and thin slices
3–4 thin slices fresh ginger root, peeled
3–4 spring onions, cut into 2-inch
  (5-cm) sections, white and green
  parts separated
2–3 teaspoons thin soy sauce

The choice of vegetables to stir-fry together is really up to you. Be imaginative: give the dish a visual appeal; also make some contrast of texture among the vegetables. Take this recipe as a guideline and add or subtract a vegetable as you like. When the vegetables are leafy and tender, there is no need to blanch them either.

1. Pour a kettle of water into the wok and bring to the boil. Add 1½ teaspoons of the salt and 1½ tablespoons of the oil. Add the green beans, return to the boil, then continue to blanch for about 2 minutes. Add the cabbage, carrots and bamboo shoots, return to the boil then continue to cook for 2 more minutes. Pour into a colander and refresh under cold running water in order to retain the crispness and vivid colour of the vegetables. Drain. (This step can be done a couple of hours in advance.)

2. Dry the wok. Reheat over a high heat until smoke rises. Add the remaining 3½ tablespoons of oil and swirl it around. Add the ginger, stir, then add the white spring onion and stir a few times. Return all the vegetables to the wok and, going to the bottom of the wok with the wok scoop or metal spatula, turn and toss for about 2 minutes or until the vegetables are tender yet still crunchy. Adjust the heat if the cabbage begins to burn. Season with the remaining ½ teaspoon salt and the soy sauce. Add the green spring onion. Remove on to a serving dish and serve hot.

SAUTÉING

The Chinese were using the frying cooking method by Han times (206 BC–AD 220), even though it may not have been exactly the same as modern sautéing or shallow-fat frying.

Related to deep-frying and stir-frying, sautéing is nevertheless distinctively different from them. In deep-frying so much oil is used that the pieces of food being deep-fried can actually swim in it, but in sautéing a comparatively small amount of oil is needed to cook the ingredients. True to its name, the motion of stirring is essential to stir-frying and the ingredients are cut up into fairly small morsels; in sautéing the ingredients are kept in large pieces and are fried *in situ*, turning half-way through the cooking time. If speed is called for in stir-frying, then patience is the secret of success in sautéing. The food is fried slowly over a modest heat until its surface gradually turns the golden brown colour it should be.

While the French sauté pans, deep with a flat bottom, are excellent, the Chinese wok, with its quick and even distribution of heat, comes up to the mark as well. Do not hesitate to tilt the wok to this side or that in order to concentrate on frying a particular section of a large ingredient. The Chinese would sauté a whole fish, with head and tail, in the wok. Naturally, the flame is concentrated in the centre so the only way to get the fish evenly brown is to use the tilting method.

Start shallow-frying with about half the oil and dribble in more oil around the ingredients as you go along or when you turn the food over. To add to the fragrance you can splash in some rice wine or medium dry sherry towards the end of the cooking time, just as you would for stir-frying.

Sauté Halibut

1 or 2 halibut steaks, about 1 lb (450 g)
1½–2 teaspoons fresh ginger juice (see
  page 15)
about 2 tablespoons potato flour or
  cornflour
½ teaspoon salt
3–4 tablespoons vegetable oil
2 cloves garlic, peeled and finely
  chopped
1 tablespoon Shaoxing wine or
  medium dry sherry
about ½ inch (1 cm) fresh ginger root,
  peeled and finely chopped
2 spring onions, cut into small rounds

FOR THE SAUCE mix together
1 teaspoon potato flour or 1⅓
  teaspoons cornflour
6 tablespoons water
1 tablespoon thin soy sauce
2 teaspoons rice or white wine vinegar
¼–½ teaspoon sugar

The flavour of halibut is so delicate that it deserves an equally subtle sauce like this one, which has a very slight sweet and sour taste to it. Halibut is very expensive so on lean days use cod steaks.

1. Pat the halibut steaks dry. Rub all over with the ginger juice, piercing the flesh with a fork for better absorption. Leave to stand for 10–15 minutes.
2. Just before heating the wok, press the steaks on both sides with the potato flour or cornflour, smoothing with fingers to coat evenly. Shake off excess flour.
3. Heat the wok over a high heat until smoke rises. Sprinkle with the salt, add 2 tablespoons of the oil and swirl it around. Lower the steaks into the oil and shallow fry each side for 1–2 minutes until golden. Add the garlic and ginger to the oil, let sizzle for a few seconds then splash in the wine or sherry around the side of the wok. When the sizzling subsides, trickle 1–2 tablespoons of oil around the fish, loosening the edges with the wok scoop or a metal spatula. Lower the heat, put on the wok cover and continue to cook each side for 4–5 minutes. The steaks are cooked when the flesh comes away, albeit slightly, from the main bone in the centre. Remove on to a serving dish, leaving a little oil behind in the wok.
4. Add the well-stirred sauce and the spring onion to the wok and stir until it thickens. Scoop the sauce over the fish and serve immediately.

Sauté Skate

1 lb (450 g) skate wing, skinned on one
    side
1 teaspoon fresh ginger juice (see page
    15)
about 3 tablespoons potato flour or
    cornflour
6 tablespoons vegetable oil
½ teaspoon salt
2–3 spring onions, cut into small
    rounds

FOR THE SAUCE mix together
1½ tablespoons thin soy sauce
½ teaspoon sugar
2 teaspoons Worcestershire sauce
1½ teaspoons Shaoxing wine or
    medium dry sherry
1 tablespoon water

Skate is a rather bland fish and its flesh is not oily either.
The sautéing process and the robust sauce, however,
bring it to life and make it into a good and economical
dinner for two.

1. Pat the fish dry. Rub the ginger juice over the skinless side of the skate and leave to stand for 15 minutes.
2. Coat the skate on both sides with the potato flour or
cornflour, shaking off excess flour.
3. Heat the wok over a high heat until smoke rises. Add
4 tablespoons of the oil and swirl it around several
times. Add the salt. Lower the skate, skinless side
down, into the oil and fry for about 1 minute. Loosening
the edges with the wok scoop or a metal spatula, turn
the fish over and fry the other side for about 1 minute.
Turn back to the skinless side and continue to sauté over
a moderate heat for about 6–7 minutes or until a thin
golden crust is formed. Turn over and sauté the skinned
side for about the same length of time, adding 1 tablespoon oil around the fish. The skate should be cooked
by now, the flesh flaking easily away from the main
bone. Remove to a serving dish.
4. Add the sauce and spring onion rounds to the wok
and bring to a simmer. Stir in the remaining 1 tablespoon oil, then pour over the skate. Serve immediately.

Fish Cake with Broccoli

2–3 tablespoons dried shrimps, about
  ½ oz (15 g) (see page 12)
12 oz (350 g) skinned and boned
  haddock fillet, minced
2 teaspoons salt
3 teaspoons potato flour or 4 teaspoons
  cornflour
3 tablespoons egg white, lightly beaten
6–8 turns white pepper mill
1½ teaspoons minced fresh ginger root
3–4 spring onions, cut into small
  rounds
2 long green chillies, seeded and cut
  into small rounds
7 tablespoons vegetable oil
8–12 oz (225–350 g) broccoli, trimmed
  and cut into large bite-sized pieces
2–3 thin slices fresh ginger root, peeled
1 tablespoon Shaoxing wine or
  medium dry sherry

FOR THE SAUCE mix together
1 teaspoon potato flour or 1⅓
  teaspoons cornflour
1 teaspoon thick soy sauce
1–1½ tablespoons oyster sauce (see
  page 13)
6 tablespoons stock or water

An excellent summer dish when the hot weather dampens your appetite for meat. If dried shrimps are not available, 1–2 oz (25–50 g) of minced ham can be used as a substitute. Also, many other vegetables such as Chinese cabbage, spinach, *mange-tout*, bean sprouts, etc, can be used instead of broccoli. In a Chinese restaurant these fish cakes would be listed in the menu as a 'Speciality Dish'. Although they are not difficult to make, they do require a little time. You can always make them in two stages: you can either make up the lump of fish paste in advance and refrigerate it for a while, or you can make the paste into fish cakes and then keep them in the refrigerator for one or two days before cutting into finger-sized pieces and frying.

1. Rinse the shrimps. Pour over just enough very hot water to cover and leave to stand for 15–20 minutes. Drain. Mince in a food processor or finely chop by hand.
2. Prepare the fish paste. Put the minced haddock in a bowl. Add 1 teaspoon of the salt and stir vigorously in the same direction for about 1 minute until gelatinous in texture. Sprinkle with the potato flour or cornflour, add the egg white then stir again until the fish mixture becomes one sticky lump again. Add the pepper, ginger, spring onion and chilli and stir to mix well. Divide into 2 equal lumps.
3. Blanch the broccoli. Bring half a wokful of water to the boil, add the remaining 1 teaspoon salt and 1 tablespoon of the oil. Add the broccoli, return to the boil and continue to cook for 3–4 minutes or until it is tender yet still has a bite to it. Pour into a colander and refresh under cold running water. Drain.
4. Reheat the wok over a high heat until smoke rises. Add 2 tablespoons oil and swirl it around. Add 1 lump of the fish paste and immediately flatten it with the wok scoop or metal spatula to a circular cake about 7 inches (18 cm) in diameter. Fry for about 30 seconds, lower the

heat to medium and fry for another 60 seconds. Flip over and fry the other side the same way. Both sides of the fish cake should be golden brown but not burned. Remove on to a plate and keep warm nearby.

5. Turn up the heat again and add 2 tablespoons oil. Fry the remaining lump of fish paste as before. Wash and dry the wok.

6. Cut the fish cakes into finger-sized pieces.

7. Reheat the wok over a high heat until smoke rises. Add 1 tablespoon oil and swirl it around. Add the ginger slices, stir a few times then lower the heat to medium. Return the broccoli to the wok and stir until thoroughly hot. Remove on to a warm serving dish.

8. Reheat the wok until smoke rises. Add the remaining 1 tablespoon oil and swirl it around. Return the fish pieces and flip and turn until very hot again. Splash the wine or sherry round the side of the wok and, when the sizzling dies down, pour in the well-stirred sauce, continuing to stir as the sauce thickens. Remove and spread on the broccoli. Serve immediately.

Note: the fish cakes can be made ahead and kept in the refrigerator for up to 2 days.

Whiting with Sweet and Sour Sauce

1 whiting, about 1½ lb (700 g),
  cleaned but with the head left on
¾–1 teaspoon salt
1 tablespoon fresh ginger juice (see
  page 15)
several tablespoons potato flour or
  cornflour
6 tablespoons vegetable oil
2–3 thin slices fresh ginger root, peeled
1 inch (5 cm) fresh ginger root, peeled
  and finely chopped
2–3 fresh red or green chillies, cut into
  small rounds (optional)
3–4 spring onions, cut into small
  rounds, white and green parts
  separated

FOR THE SAUCE mix together
1½ teaspoons potato flour or 2
  teaspoons cornflour
4 tablespoons rice vinegar or white
  wine vinegar
4 tablespoons sugar
¾ teaspoon salt
2 teaspoons concentrated tomato purée
1 tablespoon thin soy sauce
1½ teaspoons Worcestershire sauce
1½ tablespoons Shaoxing wine or
  medium dry sherry
6–7 tablespoons water

Whiting, an economical but meaty white fish with only a large bone in the centre, is rather bland on its own. This vinegary sweet and sour sauce is just the answer, for it gives zest to the overall taste, thus upgrading the fish from a homely dish to one fit for entertaining as well.

1. Pat dry the whiting. Make 2 slashes about 1 inch (5 cm) apart across both sides of the thickest part of the fish, but without going all the way to the sides. Rub all over with the salt and ginger juice, including the cavity. Leave to stand for about 15 minutes.
2. Sprinkle over both sides of the fish with a thin layer of potato flour or cornflour, shaking off excess flour. This helps to keep the skin intact when fried.
3. Heat the wok over a high heat until abundant smoke rises. Add 3 tablespoons of the oil and swirl it around the sloping edges as high as possible. Add the ginger slices, fry until burned then discard. Lower the heat to medium and add the fish. Fry for about 8–9 minutes, tilting the wok back and forth so that the whole length of the fish can be browned evenly. Slip the wok scoop or metal spatula underneath the fish to loosen edges, then carefully turn it over and fry the other side for 8–9 minutes, adding another tablespoon oil around the fish. The fish should be cooked by now. Remove on to a serving dish. Wash and dry the wok.
4. Reheat over a high heat until smoke rises. Add the remaining 2 tablespoons oil and swirl it around. Add the chopped ginger, chilli (if used) and white spring onion and stir to release their aroma. Remove the wok from the heat for about 10 seconds. Now add the well-mixed sauce, stir continuously over a gentle heat until it thickens, then boil fiercely. Scoop over the fish and serve immediately.

Ham Chow-mein (Sautéing: page 70).

Lemon Sole with Sweet and Sour Sauce (Deep-frying: page 82).

Madame So's Wok-roast Chicken
(Braising: page 88).

Prawn Toasts (Deep-frying: page 77).

All the dishes were cooked for photography by Yan-kit So and photographed by John Lee (except 32/33 right, which was photographed by Theo Bergström).

Wok-fried Fillet Steak

1 lb (450 g) fillet steak, trimmed and
    cut into pieces about ⅓–½ inch
    (8–10 mm) thick
4½ tablespoons vegetable oil
2–3 cloves garlic, peeled and crushed
    but left whole
1½ tablespoons Shaoxing wine or
    medium dry sherry
2 medium-sized onions, peeled and
    sliced
salt to taste

FOR THE MARINADE
¼ teaspoon salt
1 tablespoon thick soy sauce
1 teaspoon Worcestershire sauce
8 turns black pepper mill

My father, although his palate was almost exclusively Cantonese, to the extent that he even considered a Peking Duck 'foreign', nevertheless enjoyed a beef steak from time to time either at home or in a Western restaurant in Hong Kong. According to him, a steak should be tasty, fragrant and tender. He introduced this steak to his eight children at a tender age, and we all loved it. I have often cooked it for my son who is half Chinese and half American, and he, too, loves it.

1. Marinate the steak. Smash the steaks once with the broadside of a Chinese cleaver or a large knife to loosen the fibres. Add the salt, soy sauce, Worcestershire sauce and pepper and leave to stand for 30–45 minutes.
2. Heat the wok over a high heat until smoke rises. Add 3 tablespoons of the oil and swirl it around. Add the crushed cloves of garlic, let sizzle and turn brown releasing its aroma to the oil. Remove the garlic with a perforated spoon and discard.
3. Add the steaks to the oil and fry each side for about 15 seconds. Splash in the wine or sherry around the side of the wok. When the sizzling subsides, lower the heat to medium and continue to fry the steaks for another 15–45 seconds, depending on how you like your steak. Remove to a serving platter and keep warm, leaving some oil in the wok.
4. Add the remaining oil and the onion to the wok. Stir and turn over medium high heat for about 1 minute. Season with salt to taste then remove to the serving platter. Serve immediately.

Bean Curd with Pork

4 cakes bean curd, quartered

1 piece boneless pork, about 6 oz
(175 g), ½ inch (1 cm) thick, cut
into slivers about ⅛ inch (3 mm)
wide

4 tablespoons vegetable oil

2 cloves garlic, peeled and cut into
slivers

2 spring onions, cut into 1-inch
(2.5-cm) sections, white and green
parts separated

1 tablespoon Shaoxing wine or
medium dry sherry

FOR THE MARINADE

¼ teaspoon salt

¼ teaspoon sugar

2 teaspoons thick soy sauce

4 turns white pepper mill

1 teaspoon Shaoxing wine or medium
dry sherry

½ teaspoon potato flour or ¾ teaspoon
cornflour

2 teaspoons vegetable oil

FOR THE SAUCE

½ teaspoon potato flour or ¾ teaspoon
cornflour

3 tablespoons water

1 teaspoon thick soy sauce

Each piece of bean curd has an ever-so-thin crust, all the more delightful a contrast to the melting curd consistency inside. The blandness of the bean curd against the well-seasoned pork and sauce is yet another delight to the palate.

1. Put the bean curd pieces on 2–3 changes of kitchen paper to absorb excess water, handling them with care so as not to break them.

2. Marinate the pork. Add the salt, sugar, soy sauce, pepper, wine or sherry and flour. Mix well to coat. Leave to stand for about 20 minutes. Blend in the oil.

3. Prepare the sauce. Dissolve the potato or cornflour in the water, and add the soy sauce and stir well.

4. Heat the wok over a high heat until smoke rises. Add the oil, swirl it around and wait until you see the first sign of smoke. Carefully add half of the bean curd and shallow fry for about 1 minute. Turn each piece over and fry the other side for the same amount of time. The bean curd should not stick to the bottom of the wok. Remove with a perforated metal spoon to a serving plate, draining as much oil back into the wok as possible. Fry the remaining bean curd as before and remove to a serving plate.

5. Add the garlic to the remaining oil in the wok. Let it sizzle for a few seconds then add the white spring onion and stir a few times. Add the pork and, going to the bottom of the wok with the spatula, turn and toss for about 30 seconds or until the pork is partially cooked. Splash the wine or sherry around the side of the wok, continuing to stir as it sizzles. Add the well-stirred sauce and stir as it thickens. Add the green spring onion, then remove the mixture and spread over the bean curd. Serve immediately.

Pork Escalopes

12 oz (350 g) boneless pork, leg joint,
  cut into large chop-size pieces about
  1/3 inch (8 mm) thick
2 teaspoons potato flour or 2 1/2
  teaspoons cornflour
4 tablespoons vegetable oil
2 medium onions, about 6–8 oz
  (175–225 g), peeled and cut
  lengthways into pieces
salt
6 cloves garlic, peeled but left whole

FOR THE MARINADE
1/4 teaspoon salt
1/4 teaspoon sugar
1 tablespoon thin soy sauce
6 turns white or black pepper mill
1 teaspoon Worcestershire sauce
2 teaspoons Shaoxing wine or medium
  dry sherry

FOR THE SAUCE mix together
3/4 teaspoon potato flour or 1 teaspoon
  cornflour
1 teaspoon thin soy sauce
1 teaspoon thick soy sauce
2 teaspoons tomato purée
1 tablespoon hoisin sauce (see page 13)
5 tablespoons water

This typical modern Chinese family dish reflects the foothold Western influence has gained on the Chinese cuisine in the 20th century. Conversely, the *mélange* of Chinese and Western condiments and the use of onion ('foreign onion' in Chinese) may be regarded as how the Chinese assimilate Western food into their own diet.

1. Marinate the pork. Add the salt, sugar, soy sauce, pepper, Worcestershire sauce and wine or sherry to the pork and mix thoroughly. Leave to stand for 1–2 hours, turning the pieces over occasionally.
2. Just before ready to cook, coat with the potato flour or cornflour.
3. Heat the wok over a high heat until smoke rises. Add 1 tablespoon of the oil and swirl it around. Add the onion, season with salt to taste and turn and toss continuously for about 5 minutes over a low to medium heat until the onion is partially brown around the edges yet still has a bite to it. Remove and keep warm nearby. Wash and dry the wok.
4. Reheat wok over a high heat until smoke rises. Add 2 tablespoons oil and swirl it around several times. Add the garlic, let sizzle for a few seconds then add half of the pork and fry over a medium heat for about 2–3 minutes. Loosen the edges, turn over and fry the other side for another 2–3 minutes. The pork should be cooked to a turn by now. Remove to a warm serving dish, leaving the garlic and as much oil as possible behind in the wok.
5. Add the remaining 1 tablespoon oil and swirl it around. Add the remaining pork and fry as before. Discard the burned garlic.
6. Pour into the wok the well-stirred sauce, stir to amalgamate with the remaining oil until it thickens, bubbling in a whirlpool. Return the onion to the wok and heat with the sauce until piping hot. Scoop on to the pork and serve hot.

Lemon Chicken

3 skinned and boned chicken breasts,
  about 12 oz (350 g)
1 large egg yolk
3–4 tablespoons cornflour
6 tablespoons vegetable oil

FOR THE MARINADE
½ teaspoon salt
1 teaspoon sugar
6 turns white pepper mill
2 teaspoons Shaoxing wine or medium
  dry sherry
2½–3 tablespoons fresh lemon juice

FOR THE SWEET AND SOUR SAUCE
1½ tablespoons lemon juice
1½ tablespoons sugar
½ teaspoon salt
1 teaspoon thin soy sauce
1 tablespoon tomato ketchup
1½ teaspoons cornflour
6 tablespoons water
1 tablespoon vegetable oil

FOR THE SPICED SALT
See page 14

Refreshing with a lemony taste, this Cantonese dish is
very popular in Hong Kong, especially in the summer.
The spiced salt is the authentic accompaniment, while
the sauce, with its sweet and sour appeal to palates
universally, has gained too indomitable a foothold to be
ignored.

1. Cut each chicken breast crossways into 3. With either
the broadside of a cleaver or a mallet, pound the meat
2–3 times to loosen the fibres. Put into a dish.
2. Marinate the chicken. Add the salt, sugar, pepper,
wine or sherry and lemon juice to the chicken. Leave to
stand for 1 hour or longer, turning over from time to
time and piercing the pieces for better absorption of the
marinade.
3. Prepare the sauce. Mix together the lemon juice,
sugar, salt, soy sauce, ketchup, cornflour and water.
Pour into a saucepan (or a second wok) and slowly bring
to a simmer, stirring as the sauce thickens. Remove
from the heat and stir in the oil.
4. Drain the chicken and put into another dish. Coat
with the egg yolk and roll each piece in the cornflour,
shaking off any excess.
5. Heat the wok over a high heat until smoke rises. Add
the oil and swirl it around. Add half of the chicken,
piece by piece, and do not allow them to stick together.
Fry over a medium heat for about 1–1½ minutes each
side or until just cooked, crisp and golden outside.
Remove to a serving plate. Fry the remainder in the
same oil.
6. To serve, place both the spiced salt and the sweet
and sour sauce, reheated at the last moment, on the
table and let everybody help themselves.

Chicken Thighs with Ham

8 pieces skinned and boned chicken
  thigh, about 1 lb (450 g)
4 thin whole slices prosciutto (Parma
  ham), halved
½ teaspoon salt
white pepper to taste
1½ tablespoons egg white, lightly
  beaten
a little potato flour or cornflour
3–4 tablespoons vegetable oil
3 tablespoons medium or cream
  sherry, or Shaoxing wine

This recipe is both Chinese and Italian in flavour and technique, inspired by the discovery of packaged skinned and boned chicken thighs in British supermarkets. It is a quick and tasty recipe. If it were made in China, the crimson Jinhua ham from Eastern China or Yunnan ham from Western China would be used instead of prosciutto. But as neither of these are easy to come by (if ever) in the West, I have been amazed by how reminiscent prosciutto is of the two Chinese hams.

1. Cut through the middle of each piece of chicken and place 1 half-piece of prosciutto, folded snugly to fit, on one side. Fold up each chicken thigh again.
2. Sprinkle the chicken thighs with salt and pepper to taste. Coat with the egg white and sieve all over with a thin layer of potato flour or cornflour.
3. Heat the wok over a high heat until smoke rises. Add the oil and swirl it around. Add the chicken thighs and brown each side for about 1–1½ minutes. Splash in the sherry or Shaoxing wine around the side of the wok and, when the sizzling is less fierce, lower the heat to medium, put on the wok cover and continue to cook for about 6 minutes. Turn the pieces over and cook, covered, for about another 6 minutes. The chicken thighs should be cooked by now, brown outside but tender inside with most of the juices sealed in, leaving almost pure but fragrant oil around them.

Ham Chow-mein

6 oz (175 g) dried Chinese egg noodles
5 tablespoons vegetable oil
3–4 spring onions, cut diagonally into thin slices, white and green parts separated
3–4 sticks celery, cut diagonally into thin slices, or 3 oz (75 g) canned bamboo shoots, drained and sliced
4 oz (100 g) ham, cut into thin rectangular strips

FOR THE SAUCE mix together
¼ teaspoon salt
1 tablespoon thick soy sauce
1½ teaspoons potato flour or 2 teaspoons cornflour
6 fl oz (175 ml, ¾ cup) water

Chow-mein (stir-fried noodles) has become a household name in the West ever since the Chinese emigrants in San Francisco spread the word in the last century. To achieve the best effect, however, one does not stir-fry the noodles but fry them, creating a toasted surface on both sides and a tender soft inside. Add to this a topping of meat and vegetables with a sauce seeping through the crusty to the tender and we have a scrumptious lunch.

1. Plunge the noodles into a large pot of boiling water, return to the boil and continue to cook for about 4 minutes or until *al dente*, separating the noodles with a pair of chopsticks or a fork. Pour into a colander and refresh under cold running water. Drain thoroughly and leave in the colander for 1–2 hours.
2. Heat the wok over a high heat until smoke rises. Add 3 tablespoons of the oil, swirl it around and wait until smoke rises. Add the noodles and spread them out so that the surface will be about 8 inches (20 cm) across. Brown the bottom over a medium-high to high heat for 3–4 minutes, peeping to check if they become too brown after the first 2 minutes. Loosen the edges all round and flip the 'noodle cake' over and brown the other side as before, adding 1 tablespoon oil around the side of the wok. Transfer to a warm serving dish and keep nearby.
3. Add the remaining oil to the wok and swirl it around. Add the white spring onion and stir a few times. Add the celery or bamboo shoots and stir for 30–60 seconds until thoroughly hot. Add the ham and stir until hot. Push the ingredients to the sides of the wok, lower the heat to medium and pour the well-stirred sauce into the centre. As the sauce thickens, stir in the surrounding ingredients, add the green spring onion then scoop the mixture and sauce over the noodles. Serve immediately.

Chicken Chow-mein

8 oz (225 g) dried Chinese egg noodles
6 oz (175 g) skinned and boned chicken
breast fillet, cut into matchstick-
sized pieces
8 tablespoons vegetable oil
4–6 medium-sized Chinese
mushrooms, reconstituted (see page
14) and cut into very thin pieces
3 sticks celery, cut diagonally into thin
pieces
pinch of salt
2–3 cloves garlic, peeled and finely
chopped
3 spring onions, cut into 1-inch
(2.5-cm) sections, white and green
parts separated
1 tablespoon Shaoxing wine or
medium dry sherry

FOR THE MARINADE
¼ teaspoon salt
¼ teaspoon sugar
2 teaspoons thin soy sauce
6 turns white pepper mill
1–2 teaspoons Shaoxing wine or
medium dry sherry
1 teaspoon cornflour
1 tablespoon egg white
1½ teaspoons vegetable oil

FOR THE SAUCE mix together
¼ teaspoon salt
1 tablespoon thick soy sauce
1½ teaspoons potato flour or 2
teaspoons cornflour
6 fl oz (175 ml, ¾ cup) water

Here is another chow-mein using chicken instead of
ham. With the chicken there is obviously a bit more
work involved as the meat needs to be marinated.

1. Proceed as step 1 opposite.
2. Marinate the chicken. Add the salt, sugar, soy sauce,
pepper and wine or sherry to the chicken and stir to
coat. Sprinkle with the cornflour, add the egg white and
stir again to coat evenly. Leave to stand for about 20
minutes. Blend in the oil.
3. Fry the noodles as in step 2 opposite.
4. Add 1 tablespoon oil to the wok and swirl it around.
Add the Chinese mushroom, stir a few times, then add
the celery, season with a pinch of salt and stir for 1–2
minutes over a medium-high heat until thoroughly hot.
Remove to a serving dish and keep warm nearby. Wash
and dry the wok.
5. Reheat the wok over a high heat until smoke rises.
Add 3 tablespoons oil and swirl it around. Add the
garlic, let sizzle, then the white spring onion and stir a
few times. Add the chicken and, going to the bottom of
the wok with the wok scoop or metal spatula, flip and
turn for 30–60 seconds or until the chicken is becoming
opaque. Splash the wine or sherry around the side of
the wok, continuing to stir as it sizzles. Remove to a
dish.
6. Lower the heat, add the well-stirred sauce, stirring as
it thickens. Return the celery mixture and chicken to the
wok and add the green spring onion. Stir to mix, then
scoop the ingredients and sauce over the noodles. Serve
immediately.

Sauté Pouch Eggs

about 3 tablespoons vegetable oil
4 large eggs
salt to taste
1 tablespoon thin or thick soy sauce

To be expected, fried eggs can be done in the wok. The Chinese actually do fry their eggs in the wok. Even though they have to be fried individually, the central well of the wok helps to give the fried eggs the perfect round shape – wallet pouches as the Chinese call them – otherwise difficult to achieve in a flat frying pan. The Chinese sometimes eat Pouch Eggs as a side dish when unexpected guests arrive and another dish is needed. A pouch egg is put on top of the rice in the bowl and the yolk, flavoured with soy sauce, gives added taste to the rice and makes it more interesting.

1. Heat the wok over a high heat until smoke rises. Add 1 tablespoon of the oil and swirl it around. Reduce the heat to medium and add 1 egg to the oil. Shallow fry it for about 1 minute or until the edges are crinkly and pale golden. Sprinkle with a little salt to taste. Slide the wok scoop or a metal spatula underneath the egg and carefully fold half of the egg over, covering the yolk. Flip the egg over and fry the other side for anything between 10–60 seconds, depending on how runny you like the yolk. Remove to a serving plate and keep warm nearby.
2. Add 1–1½ teaspoons oil to the wok and reheat over a medium heat. Add another egg and fry as before. When all the eggs are done and removed to the serving plate, pour over the soy sauce. Serve immediately.

Sauté Stuffed Bean Curd

6 cakes firm bean curd, each about
    2½ inches (6.5 cm) square and
    1¼ inches (3 cm) thick
4 oz (100 g) skinned and boned
    haddock fillet, minced
⅓ teaspoon salt
1 teaspoon cornflour
1½ tablespoons egg white, lightly
    beaten
4 turns white pepper mill
1 teaspoon minced fresh ginger root
1 oz (25 g) ham, minced
6 tablespoons vegetable oil
3 thin slices fresh ginger root, peeled
2 teaspoons sesame oil

FOR THE SAUCE mix together
1 teaspoon potato flour or 1⅓
    teaspoons cornflour dissolved in 1
    tablespoon water
2 teaspoons Shaoxing wine or medium
    dry sherry
1 teaspoon thick soy sauce
2 tablespoons oyster sauce (or 1⅓
    tablespoons thick soy sauce)
6 tablespoons chicken stock

Stuffing the fragile bean curd may seem like a difficult task, but in fact it isn't, so take heart and try it.

1. Steep the bean curd in hot water for about 15 minutes. Drain, handling with care to keep each cake whole. Cut each cake into 3 slices. Lay the rectangular slices flat on changes of kitchen paper to absorb excess water.
2. Prepare the stuffing. Put the minced haddock in a bowl. Add the salt and stir vigorously in the same direction for about 1 minute until gelatinous in texture. Sprinkle with cornflour, add the egg white, then stir until the fish mixture becomes one lump. Add the pepper, ginger and ham, stir to mix well.
3. Using a small pointed knife, cut a small rectangle in the centre of each slice of bean curd, about ⅔ × 1 inch (1.5 × 2.5 cm) and ⅕ inch (5 mm) deep. Gently scrape away this layer of bean curd and discard.
4. Into each hollow, put about 1½ teaspoons stuffing and level the stuffing with the surface of the rest of the bean curd.
5. Heat the wok over a high heat until smoke rises. Add 4 tablespoons of the oil and swirl it around. Add the ginger, let sizzle until brown then remove and discard. Add 6 slices stuffed bean curd, one at a time, stuffing side down, into the oil. Fry over a moderate heat for about 3 minutes until golden in colour. Slipping the wok scoop or metal spatula underneath the bean curd, carefully turn the slices over, one by one. Fry the other side for about 2 minutes. Remove to a serving dish, leaving behind in the wok as much oil as possible.
6. Add 1 tablespoon oil and reheat over a high heat. Add another 6 slices bean curd and fry as before. Repeat until all are done.
7. Lower the heat. Add the well-stirred sauce and stir until it comes to the boil and thickens. Scoop on to the bean curd. Sprinkle on the sesame oil and serve hot.

Sauté Potato Cakes

1 lb (450 g) potatoes, peeled and cut
　into large chunks
6 oz (175 g) pork with a little fat,
　finely minced
2 tablespoons hot water
1/2 oz (15 g) or 2 tablespoons dried
　shrimps, rinsed
about 8 tablespoons vegetable oil
2 large shallots, peeled and roughly
　chopped
2 tablespoons potato flour or 2 1/2
　tablespoons cornflour

FOR THE MARINADE
1/3–1/2 teaspoon salt
1/4 teaspoon sugar
2 teaspoons thin soy sauce
6 turns white pepper mill
2 teaspoons Shaoxing wine or medium
　dry sherry
1/2 teaspoon potato flour or 3/4 teaspoon
　cornflour
1 teaspoon sesame oil

Potato is not a staple food for the Chinese and I grew up eating it occasionally and always as one of the dishes to accompany rice. This particular one, which my aunt made so well for us at home, I find reminiscent of the Swiss rosti.

1. Boil the potato for about 15 minutes or until just cooked through. Drain well and mash, but not too finely.
2. Marinate the pork. Add the salt, sugar, soy sauce, pepper, wine or sherry and flour to the pork and stir in the same direction to mix thoroughly. Leave to stand for about 15 minutes. Blend in the oil.
3. Pour 2 tablespoons very hot water over the dried shrimps and leave to soak for about 15 minutes. Drain, then chop finely. Mix in with the pork.
4. Heat the wok over a high heat until smoke rises. Add 2 tablespoons of the oil and swirl it around. Add the shallot and stir about 6 times to release the aroma. Add the pork and, going to the bottom of the wok with the scoop or a metal spatula, turn and flip for about 30–45 seconds or until the pork is barely cooked. Remove and stir into the potato mixture, mixing well. Wash and dry the wok.
5. Stir the flour into the potato mixture. Divide into 8 portions. Flatten them, one by one, between the palms of your hands to make into round cakes, each about 2 1/2 inches (6.5 cm) across.
6. Reheat the wok over a high heat until smoke rises. Add 2 tablespoons oil and swirl it around. Lower the heat to medium and put in 4 potato cakes, taking care not to let them stick to each other. Fry for about 3–5 minutes or until golden brown in colour. Carefully turn the cakes over, one by one, and trickle around the edges about 1 tablespoon oil and fry until golden brown. Remove to a serving plate and keep warm nearby.
7. Fry the remainder as before. Serve hot.

DEEP-FRYING

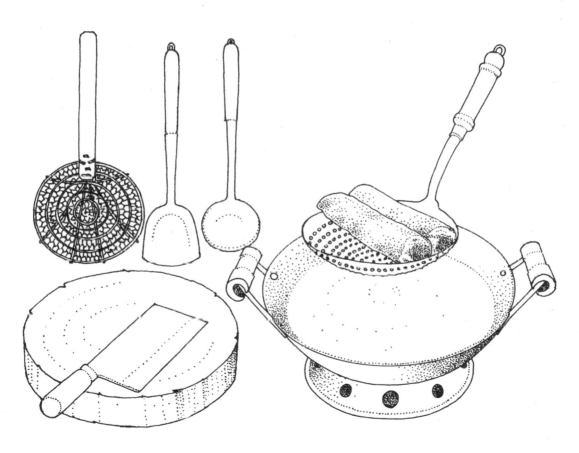

Deep-frying is a common cookery technique in the cuisines of many different nationalities, but although there are special deep-fryers in which to do the job, the Chinese have always used their versatile woks. Just as with steaming, the wok must sit securely on its stand on top of the burner before oil is poured in, filling about half-way up the sides. If the level of oil comes too far up, common sense tells you that it may easily spill over when food is added, causing a fire hazard and possible skin burns.

When it comes to heating the oil, there are several ways to test its readiness. A good old Chinese way is to throw in a small round of green spring onion; if it sizzles fiercely on the surface, the oil is hot enough. A European counterpart is the stale bread cube; the hotter the oil the shorter length of time it takes for the cube to brown. The most reliable method, especially for an inexperienced cook, is to use a special deep-frying thermometer. I use this last method whenever I deep-fry, and I have detailed the correct temperatures for all the recipes in this section.

To deep-fry Chinese food successfully in the wok you must have a perforated spoon or, better still, a large strainer in place of the Western frying basket. If possible, use a long pair of bamboo chopsticks with which to move the food around while it is cooking in order to prevent pieces sticking together, although you can always use a wooden spoon.

Always, when food is removed from the oil, put it on some of our wonderful kitchen paper to absorb any excess grease.

What is the desired effect of deep-fried food, you may well ask? It should be golden in colour to look at, the batter crisp to the bite while the ingredients inside are juicy and tender. To achieve this, a very quick second immersion in the hot oil will give an extra crispy result.

Prawn Toasts

Makes 32 pieces

*1 lb (450 g) medium-sized raw prawns
    in the shell but without heads, fresh
    or frozen (see page 13)*
1 teaspoon salt
¼ teaspoon sugar
1 teaspoon cornflour
1 egg white
2½–3 oz (70–75 g) pork fat, minced
*6–8 water chestnuts, fresh or canned,
    peeled and minced*
*8–9 pieces one-day-old white bread
    without crust*
white sesame seeds
vegetable oil for deep-frying
chilli sauce

These are not only delicious but also fun to make. What is important is to make a very light prawn paste.

1. If frozen prawns are used, defrost thoroughly. Shell and devein. Pat dry. Mince either by hand or in a food processor. Transfer to a large bowl.

2. Prepare the prawn paste. Add the salt and sugar to the minced prawn and stir in the same direction until difficult to continue. Sprinkle with the cornflour, add the egg white and stir again vigorously for 1–2 minutes or until the paste is light and fluffy in texture. Add the pork fat and water chestnut and stir to mix well. Leave in the refrigerator, covered, for 30 minutes or longer.

3. Cut each piece of bread into 4 triangles, about 2 × 2 × 2½ inches (5 × 5 × 6.5 cm). With a knife, spread all over the top of each triangle of bread some prawn paste, shaping it into a slightly sloping mound to give an attractive appearance. Leave the sides of the bread clean but smear a tiny bit of paste over the corners to stick the paste to the bread. Roll the prawn paste side of the triangles on the sesame seeds.

4. Half-fill the wok with oil and heat over a high heat until it reaches 350°F (180°C) or until a cube of stale bread foams at once. Add the triangles, paste side down, 8–10 at a time or as many as can float freely, and deep-fry for about 1½ minutes or until the corners take on colour. Turn over the triangles. As soon as the bread is golden brown, remove and drain on kitchen paper.

5. Reheat the oil to the same temperature and deep-fry the remainder as before. Remove toasts to a serving platter. Serve with the chilli sauce as a dip.

Note: deep-fried prawn toasts can be frozen. Also, if you are in a great hurry, instead of cutting a piece of bread into triangles, simply spread the prawn paste on to the whole piece. When deep-fried, cut into strips or triangles for serving.

Phoenix Rolls

**Serves 4 for lunch with a salad or
8–12 as first course**

1 quantity prawn paste (see below)
4 crêpes (see below)
*4 spring onions, 7½–8 inches
(19–20 cm) long*
2 egg whites, lightly beaten
2 egg yolks
potato flour or cornflour
vegetable oil for deep-frying

FOR THE PRAWN PASTE
*1 lb (450 g) medium-sized raw prawns
in the shell but without heads, fresh
or frozen (see page 13)*
1 teaspoon salt
1 teaspoon cornflour
1 egg white
2½–3 oz (75 g) pork fat, minced
*6–8 water chestnuts, fresh or canned,
peeled and minced*

FOR 1 CRÊPE
1 large egg
*¾ teaspoon potato flour or 1 teaspoon
cornflour mixed with 1 teaspoon
water to a paste*
small pinch salt
1 tablespoon vegetable oil

These rolls undoubtedly belong to the realm of Chinese *haute cuisine*, involving as they do multi-process cooking and cookery technique. The end result is one of grand simplicity, well deserving the accolade of the name 'phoenix', an emblem of royalty and beauty in traditional China.

1. Prepare the prawn paste. If frozen prawns are used, defrost thoroughly. Shell and devein the prawns. Pat dry. Mince either by hand or in a food processor. Transfer to a large bowl.
2. Add the salt and stir in the same direction until difficult to continue. Sprinkle with the cornflour, add the egg white and stir again vigorously for 1–2 minutes or until the paste is light and fluffy in texture. Add the pork fat and water chestnuts and stir well to mix. Leave in the refrigerator, covered, for 30 minutes or longer.
3. Meanwhile prepare the crêpes. Beat 1 egg lightly, then beat in the potato flour or cornflour paste until homogenized. Season with salt. Heat an 8-inch (20-cm) flat frying pan, preferably non-stick, over a moderate heat until hot. Add 1 tablespoon oil, swirl it around to reach the sides, then pour off half of it. Pour in the egg and tip the pan making sure it reaches the edges in one even layer. Fry over a low heat until set but not brown. Carefully loosening the edges with a metal spatula, flip the crêpe over and fry the other side until set. Remove to a flat plate or surface and let cool.
4. Repeat this process until all 4 crêpes are made.
5. Divide the prawn paste into 4 equal portions. Using your fingers, spread 1 portion evenly over half of the crêpe, stopping just short of the circular edge. Place 1 spring onion across the centre of the crêpe next to the prawn paste. Again using your fingers (or a pastry brush), smear egg white on the other half of the crêpe, going to the circular edge as well.

6. Pick up the half with prawn paste and roll away from your body into a sausage – the Phoenix Roll. The egg white on the other half will seal the roll.

7. Repeat until all 4 rolls are done.

8. Put the rolls, 2 at a time, on to a lightly oiled heat-proof dish and steam them in the wok (see page 24) for 10–12 minutes until the prawn paste is cooked. Remove from the dish and let cool for a few minutes. Wash and dry the wok.

9. Brush each roll with egg yolk then roll, one by one, over the potato flour or cornflour until evenly coated. Shake off excess flour, if necessary.

10. Half-fill the wok with oil and heat over a high heat until it reaches the temperature of 350°F (180°C), or until a cube of stale bread browns in 60 seconds. Lower the rolls into the oil and deep-fry them for about 4 minutes or until golden in colour, turning them over from time to time. Remove with a large perforated strainer, then immerse them in the oil again for about 10–20 seconds to crisp a second time. Remove and put on kitchen paper.

11. If the Phoenix Rolls are to be served as a first course or hors d'oeuvres, place them on a platter and cut diagonally into pieces about 1 inch (2.5 cm) wide. Chilli and Worcestershire sauces can be used as dips.

Smoked Halibut or Turbot

2–3 halibut or turbot steaks, about
  1¼ lb (550 g), each ½ inch (1 cm)
  thick
4–5 large leaves Iceberg lettuce, cut
  into very thin strips
3 red tomatoes, cut into thin slices
oil for deep-frying
2 tablespoons sugar
1 tablespoon black tea leaves (Chinese
  or Indian)
mayonnaise

FOR THE SPICED LIQUID
1 tablespoon vegetable oil
1½ inches (4 cm) fresh ginger root,
  peeled and crushed
2 spring onions, halved crossways
½ pint (300 ml, 1¼ cups) water
1 teaspoon salt
1 tablespoon thin soy sauce
½ teaspoon ground cinnamon or
  five-spice powder (see page 13)
1 tablespoon Shaoxing wine or
  medium dry sherry

The technique of preparing this dish is adapted from the well-known Cantonese dish called Smoked Pomfret. While pomfret, a fish of subtle taste and texture, is easily available in South China, South-east Asia and India, it is never seen fresh in Europe and North America. But cod, halibut and turbot, all available on both sides of the Atlantic Ocean, can be used successfully as substitutes. Compared to halibut and turbot, cod steaks are much more economical, while their taste and texture, unfortunately, are just as much less interesting.

1. Prepare the spiced liquid. Heat the wok over a high heat until smoke rises. Add the oil and swirl it around. Add the ginger and spring onion and stir to release their aroma. Add the water and season with the salt, soy sauce and cinnamon or five-spice powder. Bring to the boil, then continue to boil for 10–15 minutes, reducing the water to about 8 fl oz (225 ml, 1 cup). Pour the mixture into a shallow bowl and let cool to room temperature. Add the wine or sherry.
2. Pat dry the fish. Add to the spiced liquid which should almost or just cover the fish. Leave to stand for 3 hours, turning over from time to time and piercing the flesh with a sharp instrument for better absorption of the soaking liquid.
3. Between 15–30 minutes before deep-frying them, lift the fish out of the liquid and put on to a wire rack to dry off excess moisture. Discard the spiced liquid.
4. Spread the lettuce in the middle of a serving dish and arrange the tomato slices around it. Put into the refrigerator to chill until the fish is ready to be served.
5. Half-fill the wok with oil and heat to a temperature of 375°F (190°C)–400°F (200°C), or until a cube of stale bread foams fiercely immediately. Carefully lower the fish into the oil and deep-fry for about 8–10 minutes until light brown in colour, turning them over once.

Remove with a large hand strainer or perforated spoon and put on to kitchen paper.

6. Empty the oil into a container for other use. Leave the wok oily and unwashed.

7. Sprinkle the sugar into the centre of the wok, then sprinkle the tea leaves on top. Transfer the fish on to a latticed rack (wire or bamboo) which is fitted into the wok above the sugar and tea, leaving a gap of ½–1 inch (1–2.5 cm). Put on the wok lid. Turn on a high heat to produce smoke by melting the sugar and burning the tea leaves. Smoke the fish for 3–5 minutes from the time you see smoke escaping from the wok lid. Remove from the heat. (The layer of burned sugar and tea can be easily removed from the oiled wok.)

8. Place the fish on top of the lettuce in the serving plate. Serve either hot or cold. Use the mayonnaise as a dip.

Lemon Sole with Sweet and Sour Sauce

about 1½ lb (700 g) lemon sole fillets
vegetable oil for deep-frying

FOR THE BATTER
4 oz (100 g) self-raising flour
1 large egg
9 tablespoons iced water
½ teaspoon salt
1 tablespoon vegetable oil

FOR THE SAUCE
3–4 teaspoons cornflour
8 fl oz (225 ml, 1 cup) water
3 tablespoons rice or white wine
   vinegar
3–3½ tablespoons sugar
½ teaspoon salt
2 teaspoons thin soy sauce
1 teaspoon Worcestershire sauce
1 tablespoon tomato ketchup
1 tablespoon vegetable oil

The delicate texture of the lemon sole is well complimented by this very light batter.

1. Prepare the batter. Sift the flour into a mixing bowl and stir in the egg. Add the water gradually, stirring to blend into a smooth batter, like thin runny cream in consistency. Add the salt. Leave to stand for 20–30 minutes then blend in the oil to make it smoother.
2. Prepare the sauce. Dissolve the cornflour in about 2 tablespoons of the water, add the vinegar, sugar, salt, soy sauce, Worcestershire sauce and ketchup. Stir in the remaining water. Pour into a saucepan (or a second wok) and cook over a medium heat until the sauce thickens, stirring to ensure that it does not become lumpy. Remove from the heat and blend in the oil. Keep nearby.
3. Pat dry the lemon sole fillets. Halve lengthways, then cut each half crossways into 2–3 pieces.
4. Half-fill the wok with oil and heat over a high heat until it reaches a temperature of 375°F (190°C), or until a cube of stale bread browns in 50 seconds. In the meantime, add half of the fish to the batter to coat. Using a pair of bamboo chopsticks or tongs, lift the fish, piece by piece, and put into the oil to deep-fry for about 1 minute or until pale golden. (When the last piece goes into the oil, the first will be almost ready to come out.) Remove on to kitchen paper to drain. Coat and deep-fry the remaining fish as before.
5. Reheat the oil to the same temperature. Add all the fish to deep-fry a second time for about 30 seconds, crisping the batter to a turn. Remove with a large hand strainer or perforated disc on to kitchen paper, then transfer to a serving plate.
6. Reheat the sauce and pour over the fish and serve immediately. (The sauce can also be served in a bowl for individuals to use as a dip.)

Deep-fried Spareribs

1½ lb (700 g) pork spareribs, cut into
   2-inch 5-cm) pieces
1½–2 tablespoons potato flour or
   2–2½ tablespoons cornflour
oil for deep-frying
2 large cloves garlic, peeled and lightly
   crushed
4 tomatoes, cut into thin slices

FOR THE MARINADE
½ teaspoon salt
½ teaspoon sugar
1 tablespoon thin soy sauce
2 teaspoons Shaoxing wine or medium
   dry sherry

FOR THE SAUCE mix together
1 teaspoon potato flour or 1⅓
   teaspoons cornflour
5 tablespoons water
2 tablespoons Chinese red vinegar or
   red wine vinegar
2 tablespoons sugar
1 tablespoon chilli sauce
¼ teaspoon salt

These spareribs have a hot, sweet and sour sauce.

1. Remove excess fat, if any. (The fat, if rendered down, makes the best lard.) Pat dry the spareribs.
2. Marinate the spareribs. Add the salt, sugar, soy sauce and wine or sherry to the spareribs and mix thoroughly. Leave to stand for about 3–4 hours, turning them over occasionally. The marinade should be all absorbed at the end of the marinating time.
3. Just before you are ready to cook, sprinkle with the flour and mix to coat well.
4. Half-fill the wok with oil and heat to 300°F (150°C), or until a cube of stale bread foams slowly. Carefully add all the spareribs, lowering the heat to maintain a temperature of between 200–250°F (100–120°C), or until only tiny whirlpools are seen on the surface of the oil. Steep the spareribs, the thin pieces for about 10 minutes and the thick pieces for 15 minutes or until they are just cooked, separating them with a long pair of bamboo chopsticks or a wooden spoon. Remove with a large hand strainer or perforated spoon and drain on kitchen paper. This step can be done several hours ahead.
5. Reheat the oil to a temperature of 350–375°F (180–190°C). Return the spareribs to the wok and deep-fry for 1–2 minutes to crisp the outside. Remove and drain on kitchen paper. Empty the oil into a container and save for other use. Wash and dry the wok.
6. Reheat the wok over a high heat until smoke rises. Add 1 tablespoon oil and swirl it around. Add the garlic, let sizzle and take on colour, releasing the aroma. Remove from the heat and let the oil cool for about 20–30 seconds. Add the well-stirred sauce and bring to the boil over a gentle heat, stirring as it thickens. Discard the garlic.
7. Return the spareribs to the wok and mix thoroughly with the sauce. Remove to a serving dish. Arrange the tomato on either side. Serve immediately.

Crispy Skin Bean Curd

4 cakes bean curd, each usually about
   2½ inches (6.5 cm) square and
   1¼ inches (3 cm) thick
oil for deep-frying
spiced salt (see page 14)

FOR THE BATTER
2 oz (50 g) plain flour
2 tablespoons cornflour
¾ teaspoon baking powder
about 4 fl oz (110 ml, ½ cup) iced
   water
1 teaspoon salt
2 tablespoons vegetable oil

Shatin in the New Territory of Hong Kong has always been famous for this dish and at the weekend people throng there to eat it. I used to be in awe of such a gastronomic feat – a very light and crispy skin covering a velvet smooth and soft curd in the centre – until I determined to find out how to prepare it.

1. Prepare the batter. Sieve the flour, cornflour and baking powder into a fairly wide-bottomed mixing bowl. Add the water gradually, stirring vigorously to mix into a very smooth and thin batter. Test by lifting a fork from the bottom of the bowl; if the batter runs down in a continuous stream breaking into drops only at the end it is of the right consistency. Stir in the salt and leave to stand in the refrigerator for 30 minutes or longer. Blend in the oil.
2. Cut each bean curd square into 3 rectangular pieces. Dab off any excess water with absorbent paper, handling with care.
3. Half-fill the wok with oil. Heat to a temperature of 375°F (190°C)–400°F (200°C), or until a cube of stale bread foams very fast in the oil.
4. When the oil is almost ready, dip the bean curd, 2–3 pieces at a time, into the batter to coat thoroughly. Using either a pair of chopsticks or a perforated spoon, gently lift them, 1 piece at a time, from the batter (let some of the excess batter drip back into the bowl) into the oil and deep-fry for about 3–4 minutes or until golden in colour. Make sure the pieces float freely in the oil. Remove individual pieces as soon as ready with a perforated spoon and put on absorbent paper.
5. Gently plunge all the bean curd pieces together into the oil again and deep-fry a second time to crisp for about 20–30 seconds. Remove together and put on to absorbent paper.
6. Place on a serving plate and serve immediately. The spiced salt is used as a dip to individual taste.

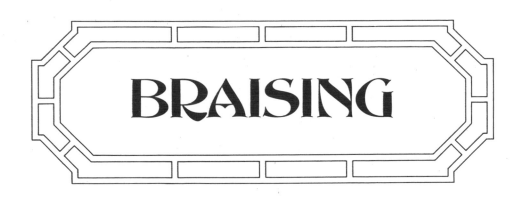

BRAISING

Braising food the Chinese way is not all that different from doing it the Western way, except in the use of seasoning and herbs. In the West, and in most other cuisines, very many different herbs and seasonings are used, whereas the Chinese very often just use star anise, a few Sichuan peppercorns, some thick soy sauce and a little rice wine or sherry. Through this grand simplicity we achieve the most sophisticated results.

Basically, the method consists of browning the main ingredient in a little fat, then cooking it in a fair amount of liquid for a long time until it is tender and richly seasoned by the sauce. A deep, heavy pot is the ideal utensil for this kind of cooking as a rule, yet the wok, complete with its spacious plateau dome cover, can be used to turn out deliciously braised dishes. It is especially suitable if the braising process is not an overly lengthy one and more in the pot-roast fashion (see Wok Roast Chicken on page 88) than it is for a stew with plenty of gravy.

When it comes to vegetables sometimes there is only a fine line between braising and stir-frying. For example, Chinese leaves can be thinly sliced and stir-fried very quickly, but if they are left in large chunks, the wok lid put on and the heat lowered, the leaves will take at least 20 minutes to become tender – and thus become a braised dish.

As in steaming, the wok lid plays an important role and should fit tightly to the sloping sides of the wok. The amount of liquid in which the food is cooked should also be checked from time to time and replenished if need be.

Braised Beef Steaks

2 tablespoons vegetable oil
2 large cloves garlic, peeled and
  crushed but kept whole
8–10 segments star anise (see page 14)
1 inch (2.5 cm) cinnamon, finely
  crushed
6 braising steaks, each about 6 oz
  (175 g) and ¾ inch (2 cm) thick,
  best with 'jelly' in the middle
2 tablespoons Shaoxing wine or
  medium dry sherry
1 tablespoon thin soy sauce
1 tablespoon thick soy sauce
½ teaspoon salt
1 teaspoon sugar
8 fl oz (225 ml, 1 cup) unseasoned beef
  or chicken stock
2 teaspoons potato flour or 2¾
  teaspoons cornflour dissolved in 3
  tablespoons water

A family dish which will go well not only with rice but also with potato and Italian pasta.

1. Heat the wok over a high heat until smoke rises. Add the oil and swirl it around. Add the garlic, let sizzle and take on colour. Adjusting the heat to medium, add the star anise and cinnamon and stir a few times. Add the steaks and brown for about 2 minutes on each side. Pour in the Shaoxing wine or sherry, turning up the heat to reduce it to half.
2. Reduce the heat again and sit the wok on its stand. Add the soy sauces, salt, sugar and the stock. Bring to a simmer. Put on the wok cover and continue to simmer for about 2¾–3 hours, so gently that at the end of the cooking time there will still be about 8 fl oz (225 ml, 1 cup) sauce in the wok with the steaks remaining whole. Turn the steaks over at the end of every hour and, if necessary, add more stock or water.
3. Remove the steaks to a serving platter and keep warm nearby. Pass the sauce through a wire sieve and discard the solids. Return the sauce to the wok, add the well-stirred dissolved potato flour or cornflour and bring to a simmer over a gentle heat, stirring until it thickens. Pour the sauce over the steaks or serve it separately.

Madame So's Wok-roast Chicken

1 cleaned chicken, 2¾–3 lb
  (1.3–1.4 kg)
1¾ teaspoons salt
10 spring onions, trimmed
5 tablespoons vegetable oil
2 tablespoons cloud ears, reconstituted
  (see pages 12 and 14) and broken
  into pieces
6 medium-sized dried Chinese
  mushrooms, reconstituted (see page
  14), and cut into very thin slices
⅓ oz (10 g) golden needles,
  reconstituted
2 tablespoons water
3 large cloves garlic, peeled and
  crushed but left whole
3 thickish slices fresh ginger root,
  peeled
8 segments (1 whole) star anise (see
  page 14)
½ teaspoon Sichuan peppercorns (see
  page 14)
8 tablespoons water

FOR THE SAUCE mix together
4 tablespoons thick soy sauce
1½ teaspoons brown sugar
1 tablespoon Shaoxing wine or
  medium dry sherry

Even though my mother, So Lam Mo-yin, is more interested in fundamentalist Christianity than food, she nevertheless produces a superb chicken dish that all her children unanimously vote to be superior to any other of its kind they have tasted anywhere. Whenever we go home to Hong Kong to visit her, she will cook this dish for us to satisfy our deprived tastebuds. Recently, upon my request, she wrote down the procedures for me in meticulous detail, which I have rendered from Chinese into English below.

1. Pat dry the chicken. Rub 1½ teaspoons of the salt all over the skin and in the cavity of the chicken and leave to stand for 30–45 minutes.
2. Meanwhile, plunge the spring onions into half a wokful of boiling water. Blanch for about 10 seconds to make them pliable. Pour into a colander and refresh them with cold water. Drain.
3. Make a knot in each of the spring onions.
4. Prepare the stuffing. Heat the wok over a high heat until smoke rises. Add 2 tablespoons of the oil and swirl it around. Add the spring onion loops, stir several times, then add the cloud ears and stir, the mushrooms and stir, and the golden needles and continue to stir for another 30 seconds. Sprinkle with 2 tablespoons of water, season with the remaining ¼ teaspoon salt and cook, covered, for about 2 minutes or until the water is absorbed. Remove the stuffing on to a plate. Wash and dry the wok.
5. Reheat the wok over a high heat until smoke rises. Add the remaining 3 tablespoons oil and swirl it around several times. Add the garlic, stir, ginger, stir, and the star anise and Sichuan peppercorns. Lower the chicken to the oil to brown over a medium heat for 4–5 minutes, turning from breast to back and side to side and taking care not to burn the condiments. Pour over the well-

stirred sauce and bring to a simmer. Remove the wok from the heat.

6. Place the stuffing into the cavity of the chicken. (This can be done either by removing the chicken to a plate or leaving it in the wok.)

7. Stand the chicken on its side in the wok. Add 4 tablespoons water and simmer fast, covered tightly, over a moderate heat for 20–25 minutes. Remove the lid, ladle the sauce over the chicken several times, turn it to stand on its other side. Add another 4 tablespoons water and continue to cook, covered, for another 20–25 minutes. Insert a chopstick into the thickest part of the thigh; if the juice which oozes out is clear, the chicken is cooked.

8. To serve it Chinese style, remove the chicken on to a chopping board. Scoop out the stuffing and place it on a serving platter. Carve the chicken through the bones into 1-inch (2.5-cm) pieces and arrange them over the stuffing. Pour the sauce, reheated to a simmer, over the chicken.

9. The chicken can also be served successfully if carved like a oven-roasted chicken in the manner you are accustomed to, and the stuffing and sauce served separately.

Braised Chicken Wings

2 lb (900 g) or 12 chicken wings,
  cleaned
½ teaspoon salt
10 turns white pepper mill
2–2½ tablespoons vegetable oil
3 cloves garlic, peeled and crushed
3 slices fresh ginger root, each about
  ⅕ inch (5 mm) thick, peeled and
  bruised
3 spring onions, cut into 2-inch (5-cm)
  sections, white and green parts
  separated
8 segments (1 whole) star anise (see
  page 14)
1½ inches (4 cm) cinnamon stick,
  crushed into bits
1 tablespoon Shaoxing wine or
  medium dry sherry

FOR THE SAUCE mix together
3½ tablespoons thick soy sauce or 2
  tablespoons thick soy and 2
  tablespoons oyster sauce (see page
  13)
4 tablespoons water
1 teaspoon sugar

Chicken wings (for that matter duck wings as well), which are not highly regarded in the West and hence inexpensive, are a Chinese gourmet's delight. Try this recipe, but remember not to chop off the pinions either.

1. Pat dry the chicken wings. Sprinkle over with the salt and pepper and leave to stand for about 30 minutes.
2. Heat the wok over a high heat until smoke rises. Add the oil and swirl it around. Add the garlic and stir, then add the ginger and white spring onion and stir to release their aroma. Add the star anise and cinnamon and stir a few more times, adjusting the heat so as not to burn the condiments. Add the chicken wings to brown gently with the condiments for about 5 minutes, turning them over frequently with the wok scoop or metal spatula. Splash in the wine or sherry around the side of the wok. When the sizzling subsides, pour in the well-stirred sauce.
3. Bring the sauce to the boil. Add the lid to the wok and continue to cook over a low to medium heat for either 30 minutes if you like the meat to be tender but firm or 60 minutes if you prefer it to be falling off the bones. In either case, turn the wings over at half time for even cooking and colouring. It may be necessary to add 3–4 tablespoons water if you choose the longer cooking period.
4. Remove the lid. Turn up the heat and add the green spring onion. Spoon the sauce in the wok over the wings continuously for 1–2 minutes. This reducing process enriches the taste and gives the sauce a slight glazing effect. Remove to a serving platter and serve hot.

Note: the chicken wings are also delicious served cold.

Duck with Pickling Onions

1 oven-ready duck, about 4½ lb (2 kg)
1 large kettle boiling water
thick soy sauce
5 tablespoons vegetable oil
12–18 pickling onions, peeled
3 tablespoons Shaoxing wine or
   medium dry sherry
1 teaspoon salt
1 teaspoon brown sugar
8 fl oz (225 ml, 1 cup) chicken stock
3 tablespoons thick soy sauce
2 whole star anise or 16 segments (see
   page 14)
2 inches (5 cm) cinnamon stick, broken
   up
8 fl oz (225 ml, 1 cup) water

Covered with a lid, the wok becomes an effective casserole for slow cooking. This braised duck, with its tender yet firm textured meat is evocative of roast duck.

1. Pour a kettle of boiling water all over the duck to scald the skin, which will shrink instantly and become glossy. This helps to keep the shape of the duck. Wipe off excess water. While the skin is still warm, brush all over with thick soy sauce to colour it.

2. Heat a wok over a high heat until smoke rises. Add the oil and swirl it around. Lower the duck into the oil to brown, breast side down first, then turn over and sideways. Fry for 4–5 minutes or until the skin takes on colour. Remove the duck and keep nearby.

3. Add the whole onions to the oil and fry over a high heat for 1–2 minutes. Lift to a plate with a perforated spoon. Remove most of the oil (which can be saved to cook vegetables like cabbage or cauliflower).

4. Return the duck to the wok. Add the wine or sherry, salt, sugar, chicken stock, 3 tablespoons thick soy sauce, star anise and cinnamon. Add also about 8 fl oz (225 ml, 1 cup) water and bring to the boil. Reduce the heat, cover with the wok lid and simmer for about 1½ hours. Add the pickling onions around the duck, replenish with a little more water or stock and continue to simmer, covered, for another hour. The duck should be tender by now.

5. Remove the onions and keep warm nearby. Turn up the heat to reduce the sauce, spooning it over the duck repeatedly until the sauce becomes thicker and glazed. Alternatively, thicken the sauce with some potato flour or cornflour (about 1 tablespoon potato flour or 1⅓ tablespoons cornflour dissolved in 2 tablespoons water for every 8 fl oz [225 ml, 1 cup] sauce).

6. Remove the duck to a serving platter and arrange the onions around it. Carve it your usual way or break it up into chunks with chopsticks as the Chinese do.

Aubergine with Bacon

4 tablespoons vegetable oil
4 oz (100 g) streaky bacon rashers, cut
  into pieces
2–3 cloves garlic, peeled and crushed
3–4 spring onions, cut into 2-inch
  (5-cm) sections, white and green
  parts separated
1¼ lb (550 g) aubergine, trimmed and
  cut into fairly large pieces
½ teaspoon salt
1 teaspoon sugar
1 tablespoon Shaoxing wine or
  medium dry sherry
1 tablespoon rice or white wine vinegar
1 tablespoon thin soy sauce
4 fl oz (100 ml, ½ cup) clear stock or
  water
1 large red pepper, about 8 oz (225 g),
  seeded and roughly chopped

The spongy meat of aubergine is inclined to absorb too much cooking fat and the result can be a greasy dish if one is not careful. A little vinegar, however, cuts the grease, and the sweet red pepper, enlivening the dark mauvy tone, gives this earthy dish harmony in taste.

1. Heat the wok over a high heat until smoke rises. Add 2 tablespoons of the oil and swirl it around. Add the bacon and stir for about 1 minute until partially cooked and fragrant.
2. Add the remaining 2 tablespoons oil. Add the garlic and white spring onion and stir to release their aroma. Add the aubergine and, going to the bottom of the wok with the wok scoop or a metal spatula, turn and toss for about 1 minute to brown the pieces. Lower the heat. Add the salt, sugar, wine or sherry, vinegar, soy sauce and stock or water. Stir to mix. Put on the wok cover and continue to cook over a low heat for about 45 minutes or until the aubergine is tender and the spongy flesh impregnated with the sauce. Check for liquid at half time and carefully turn the pieces over a few times. (The aubergine can be prepared up to this point several hours ahead.)
3. Mix in the red pepper and continue to cook, covered, for 10 more minutes. Add the green spring onion, mix, then scoop on to a serving dish and serve hot.

Note: vegetarians can simply omit the use of bacon and add instead 1 extra tablespoon oil at the beginning and perhaps 1–2 teaspoons sesame oil at the end as well.

REFERENCES

References for drawings of excavated Chinese cooking pots as shown on page 9.

1 Ma Jianxi: 'Brief Report on the Excavations of the Warring States and Western Han Tombs of Yao Xian, Shaanxi Province', *Kaogu (Archaeology)* 1959, No. 3, p. 149; Plate IV, fig. 5.

2 Jiangxi Provincial Museum: 'The Eastern Han and Eastern Wu Tombs at Nanchang in Jiangxi Province', *Kaogu* 1978, No. 3, pp. 161–62; Plate V, fig. 6.

3 Li Zhengguang: 'Excavations of Ancient Cemeteries at Shahu Qiao in Changsha', *Kaogu Xuebao (The Chinese Journal of Archaeology)* 1957, No. 4, p 62; Plate XII, fig. 10.

4 The Nanjing Museum and the Municipal Museum of Yangzhou: 'The Han Dynasty Wooden-chambered Tomb at Qilidian, Yangzhou, Jiangsu', *Kaogu* 1962, No. 8, p. 402; Plate V, fig. 3.

5 Wang Zengxin: 'The Jin and Yuan Sites in Chenghou Village, Liaoning Province', *Kaogu* 1960, No. 2, p. 43; Plate V, fig. 4.

6 Tian Jingdong: 'The Discovery of Yuan Artefacts Stored in A Cellar in Liangxiang near Beijing (Peking)', *Kaogu* 1972, No. 2, pp. 33–34.

7 Su Tianjun: 'The Liao and Jin Iron Implements Unearthed at Beijing', *Kaogu* 1963, No. 3, pp 140–44.

Reference books:

Chang, K. C. ed.: *Food in Chinese Culture: Anthropological and Historical Perspectives* (Yale University Press, 1978)

Needham, Joseph: *The Development of Iron and Steel Technology in China* (W. Heffer & Sons Limited, 1964)

Song Yingxing: *Tian Gong Kai Wu* (The Exploitation of the Works of Nature, 1637)

INDEX

Asparagus in stock 56
Aubergine with bacon 92

Bamboo shoots 12
  Steamed beef with bamboo shoots 28
Bean curd 13
  Bean curd with pork 66
  Crispy skin bean curd 84
  Family bean curd 48
  Sauté stuffed bean curd 73
Bean sprouts
  Stir-fried bean sprouts 34–5
Beans, black (soy) 13, 14
  Chicken in black bean sauce 44
  Prawns in black bean sauce 38
Beans, French
  French beans with garlic 51
Beef
  Beef meat ball soup 19
  Beef with mange-tout 39
  Beef with pineapple 40
  Braised beef steaks 87
  Family bean curd 48
  Steamed beef with bamboo shoots 28
  West Lake beef soup 20
  Wok-fried fillet steak 65
BRAISING 85–92
  Aubergine with bacon 92
  Braised beef steaks 87
  Braised chicken wings 90
  Duck with pickling onions 91
  Madame So's wok-roast chicken 88–9
Broccoli
  Chinese broccoli with ginger juice 53
  Fish cake with broccoli 62–3

Cabbage
  Stir-fried white cabbage 34–5
Cauliflower
  Stir-fried creamed cauliflower 55

Celery
  Chicken with celery and cashew nuts 45
  Stir-fried celery 34–5
Chicken
  Braised chicken wings 90
  Chicken chow-mein 71
  Chicken in black bean sauce 44
  Chicken thighs with ham 69
  Chicken with celery and cashew nuts 45
  Lemon chicken 68
  Madame So's wok-roast chicken 88–9
  Steamed chicken fillet 29
Chinese leaves 86
  Stir-fried Chinese leaf 34–5
  Stir-fried creamed cauliflower (variation) 55
Chow-mein
  Chicken chow-mein 71
  Ham chow-mein 70
Cloud ears 12, 14
Cod 80
  Sauté halibut (variation) 60
  Steamed fish 26
Courgettes
  Stir-fried courgettes 52
Crabmeat
  Stir-fried milk 47
Cucumber
  Shredded pork with cucumber 43
  Stir-fried cucumber 34–5

DEEP-FRYING 75–84
  Crispy skin bean curd 84
  Deep-fried spareribs 83
  Lemon sole with sweet and sour sauce 82
  Phoenix rolls 78–9
  Prawn toasts 77
  Smoked halibut or turbot 80–1
Dried ingredients: reconstituting 14
Duck
  Duck with pickling onions 91
  Steamed duck with a plum sauce 30

Dumplings
    Steamed *siu mai* 25

Eggs
    Sauté pouch eggs 72
    Slippery egg and shrimps 46
    Stir-fried milk 47

Fish
    Fish cake with broccoli 62–3
    Steamed fish 26
    see also Cod; Grey mullet; Haddock; Halibut;
        Lemon sole; Skate; Turbot; Whiting; *also* Sea-
        food
Five-spice powder 13

Golden needles 13, 14
Grey mullet
    Steamed fish 26

Haddock
    Fish cake with broccoli 62–3
    Sauté stuffed bean curd 73
Halibut
    Sauté halibut 60
    Smoked halibut or turbot 80–1
    Steamed fish 26
Ham
    Chicken thighs with ham 69
    Ham chow-mein 70
    Shredded pork soup 22
Hoisin sauce 13

Kidneys
    Lambs' kidneys in Marsala Sauce 41

Lemon sole with sweet and sour sauce 82

Meat *see* Beef; Chicken; Duck; Kidneys; Pork
Meat balls
    Beef meat ball soup 19
Milk
    Stir-fried milk 47
Mushrooms
    Button mushroom vinaigrette 54
    Dried Chinese black mushrooms 12, 14
    Stir-fried fresh mushrooms 34–5
    Stir-fried milk 47
Mussels
    Mussels in soup 18

Noodles 15
    Chicken chow-mein 71
    Chinese egg noodles 12
    Ham chow-mein 70
    Soup noodles with shredded pork 21

Oyster sauce 13

Phoenix rolls 78–9
Pork
    Bean curd with pork 66
    Deep-fried spareribs 83
    Pork escalopes 67
    Sauté potato cakes 74
    Shredded pork soup 22
    Shredded pork with cucumber 43
    Soup noodles with shredded pork 21
    Steamed minced pork 27
    Steamed *siu mai* 25
    Stir-fried pork with leek 42
Potatoes
    Sauté potato cakes 74
Prawns
    Phoenix rolls 78–9
    Prawn toasts 77
    Prawns in black bean sauce 38
    Raw frozen prawns 13
    Steamed *siu mai* 25

Rice 15
    Mixed fried rice 50
    Shrimp stir-fried rice 49
    Steamed rice 31
Rice sticks
    Stir-fried milk 47
Rice vinegar 13

Salt, spiced 14
Sauces 13, 14
    Plum sauce 30
    Sweet and sour sauce 64, 68, 82
SAUTÉING 58–74
    Bean curd with pork 66
    Chicken chow-mein 71
    Chicken thighs with ham 69
    Fish cake with broccoli 62–3
    Ham chow-mein 70
    Lemon chicken 68
    Pork escalopes 67
    Sauté halibut 60

SAUTÉING—cont.
   Sauté potato cakes 74
   Sauté pouch eggs 72
   Sauté skate 61
   Sauté stuffed bean curd 73
   Whiting with sweet and sour sauce 64
   Wok-fried fillet steak 65
Scallops
   Stir-fried whole scallops 36–7
Seafood *see* Crabmeat; Mussels; Prawns; Scallops;
   Shrimps; *also* Fish
Shaoxing wine 13
Shrimps
   Dried shrimps 12
   Fish cake with broccoli 62–3
   Shrimp stir-fried rice 49
   Slippery egg and shrimps 46
   Stir-fried milk 47
Sichuan peppercorns 14
Siu mai
   Steamed *siu mai* 25
Skate
   Sauté skate 61
SOUPS 16–22
   Beef meat ball soup 19
   Mussels in soup 18
   Shredded pork soup 22
   Soup noodles with shredded pork 21
   West Lake beef soup 20
Soy sauce 14
Spinach
   Stir-fried spinach 34–5
Star anise 14
STEAMING 23–31
   Steamed beef with bamboo shoots 28
   Steamed chicken fillet 29
   Steamed duck with a plum sauce 30
   Steamed fish 26
   Steamed minced pork 27
   Steamed rice 31
STIR-FRYING 32–57
   Asparagus in stock 56
   Beef with mange-tout 39

Beef with pineapple 40
Button mushroom vinaigrette 54
Chicken in black bean sauce 44
Chicken with celery and cashew nuts 45
Chinese broccoli with ginger juice 53
Family bean curd 48
French beans with garlic 51
Lambs' kidney in Marsala sauce 41
Mixed fried rice 50
Prawns in black bean sauce 38
Shredded pork with cucumber 43
Shrimp stir-fried rice 49
Slippery egg and shrimps 46
Stir-fried courgettes 52
Stir-fried creamed cauliflower 55
Stir-fried milk 47
Stir-fried mixed vegetables 57
Stir-fried pork with leek 42
Stir-fried vegetables 34–5
Stir-fried whole scallops 36–7
Sweet and sour sauce
   Lemon chicken 68
   Lemon sole with sweet and sour sauce 82
   Whiting with sweet and sour sauce 64

Thickening agents 14
Toast
   Prawn toasts 77
   Slippery egg and shrimps 46
Turbot
   Smoked halibut or turbot 80–1
   Steamed fish 26

Veal
   Lambs' kidney in Marsala sauce (variation) 41
Vegetables
   Stir-fried mixed vegetables 57
   Stir-fried vegetables 34–5

Whiting with sweet and sour sauce 64
Wonton skins 14, 17
   Steamed *siu mai* 25